T0301482

Politics for Hire

Politics for Hire
The World and Work of Policy Professionals

Stefan Svallfors

Institute for Futures Studies, Stockholm, Sweden

Cheltenham, UK • Northampton, MA, USA

Published by
Edward Elgar Publishing Limited
The Lypiatts
15 Lansdown Road
Cheltenham
Glos GL50 2JA
UK

Edward Elgar Publishing, Inc.
William Pratt House
9 Dewey Court
Northampton
Massachusetts 01060
USA

A catalogue record for this book
is available from the British Library

Library of Congress Control Number: 2020942780

This book is available electronically in the **Elgar**online
Social and Political Science subject collection
http://dx.doi.org/10.4337/9781800375192

MIX
Paper from
responsible sources
FSC
www.fsc.org   FSC® C013604

ISBN 978 1 80037 518 5 (cased)
ISBN 978 1 80037 519 2 (eBook)

Printed and bound by CPI Group (UK) Ltd, Croydon, CR0 4YY

Contents

Acknowledgements

Many people and institutions have made this book possible. The research projects on which it is based were financed by the Swedish Research Council (Grant no 421-2014-962) and the Foundation for Baltic and East European Studies (Grant no 2/16).

This funding made it possible to bring together a multidisciplinary research team of truly outstanding quality. Two post-doctoral researchers, business studies scholar Anna Tyllström and political scientist Niels Selling, both at the Institute for Futures Studies, were soon joined by my fellow sociologists Joanna Mellquist and Adrienne Sörbom based at Södertörn University. Later, we enlisted political scientist Josef Hien, who came to the Institute on what was supposed to be a short-term visit but turned out to be a years-long and still continuing informal fellowship. Janine Wedel of George Mason University also joined our team for a year-long appointment as Kerstin Hesselgren Visiting Professor (also funded by the Swedish Research Council). Last, but certainly not least, the funding allowed us to hire the best research assistant there ever was, Corrie Hammar, whose tireless efforts and boundless good humour combined with an unerring grip on the project's workflow have made this endeavour possible. In the early stages of the project I also benefited from the able research assistance of Björn Werner, who among other things conducted all the interviews with policy professionals in Brussels.

These people provided a very congenial and productive micro-environment for the project. I have learned so much from them and we always have such fun when we meet. The fact that we come from slightly different institutional and disciplinary backgrounds, I think, has been key in making the project so lively and exciting. And not once have I heard any of them complain about having to read yet another chapter draft that looked suspiciously similar to the one they gently trashed some months before ...

The broader institutional environment in which we were embedded – the Institute for Futures Studies in Stockholm – is the most creative research setting in which I have been involved. The Institute is one of the few places in the world where true and radical multidisciplinary research actually works on a day-to-day basis. Thanks for making this happen go to all the staff at the Institute, but first and foremost to its director, Gustaf Arrhenius, who has assembled a staff from 10+ countries covering 10+ scientific disciplines and made it possible for us to work together. The research colloquia at the Institute are the best I have ever participated in, and so are the small daily interactions that form the substance of any intellectual environment worth its salt.

Outside the Institute, the project has benefited from the help of a small group of advisors that have provided valuable input to the comparative aspects of the project. Daunis Auers (University of Latvia), Niamh Hardiman (University College Dublin), and Mirko Noordegraf (Utrecht University) helped me navigate unfamiliar institutional settings. They also helped me recruit research assistants – Olafs Grigus in Riga, Melika Khandanian in Dublin, and Petra Ophoff in Utrecht – who helped in compiling information on policy professionals and institutional conditions in the three countries under investigation.

Malcolm Fairbrother at my Alma Mater Umeå University and its excellent Department of Sociology acted as external commentator on the final manuscript of the book. He made me understand that I needed a sharper delineation of the actors at the centre of my book, but also helped me understand better what this book is *not* about (which is in some ways as important as knowing what it actually *is* about). I also received critical and helpful comments from a number of other readers of the final manuscript: Daunis Auers, Josef Hien, Joanna Mellquist, Bo Rothstein, Adrienne Sörbom, Niels Selling, and Anna Tyllström provided more helpful pieces of advice than I have been able to follow, but the ones I did heed have made the book much better.

A final word of thanks goes to all the policy professionals in Sweden, Brussels, Latvia, Ireland, and the Netherlands who agreed to be interviewed for this book. They are typically very busy people, so the fact that each of them took one or two hours to talk to me or my collaborators about their work and their careers should be lauded. The policy professional phenomenon is sometimes painted in somewhat dark colours in this book, but the individual policy professionals we interviewed were typically very friendly, interesting, and forthcoming. The interviews often turned into thoughtful conversations that showed that they care deeply about democracy and their own role in making democracy work.

* * *

Parts of the book have previously been published in various journals, and I thank the following journals and copyright holders for permission to include sections from the following publications:

Selling, Niels, and Stefan Svallfors. 2019. 'The Lure of Power: Career Paths and Considerations among Policy Professionals in Sweden.' *Politics & Policy* 47 (5): 984–1012. (with permission from Wiley)

Svallfors, Stefan, and Anna Tyllström. 2019. 'Resilient Privatization: The Puzzling Case of For-Profit Welfare Providers in Sweden.' *Socio-Economic Review* 17 (3): 745–765. (with permission from Oxford University Press)

Svallfors, Stefan. 2017. 'Knowing the Game: Motivations and Skills among Partisan Policy Professionals.' *Journal of Professions and Organization* 4 (1): 55–69. (with permission from Oxford University Press)

Svallfors, Stefan. 2017. '"Most MPs are Not All That Sharp". Political Employees and Representative Democracy.' *International Journal of Public Administration* 40 (7): 548–558. (with permission from Taylor & Francis)

Svallfors, Stefan. 2016. 'Out of the Golden Cage: PR and the Career Opportunities of Policy Professionals.' *Politics & Policy* 44 (1): 56–73. (with permission from Wiley)

Stockholm, 1 June 2020

1.   The new unelected

In September 2018, the embattled Trump presidency suffered yet another embarrassment. In an anonymous letter to the *New York Times*, a leading figure in the White House administration described how they had repeatedly disobeyed orders from the president and withheld crucial information from the commander-in-chief. This, they claimed, they had done in order to save the country from pending foreign policy disasters resulting from Trump's erratic and unpredictable behaviour.[1]

Some observers saw these as patriotic deeds to save the US from the dangerous actions of an unhinged president. Others were more hesitant to lend their full support to such clearly egregious acts as withholding information from the elected president. Most seemed relieved, however, that there were at least some people in the White House who had some common sense and integrity. The purported 'adults in the room' would save the US and the world.

Former president Barack Obama would have none of it. In a speech at the University of Illinois at Urbana-Champaign on 7 September 2018, he made his position clear:

> And, by the way, the claim that everything will turn out okay because there are people inside the White House who secretly aren't following the President's orders, that is not a check – I'm being serious here – that's not how our democracy is supposed to work. (Applause.) These people aren't elected. They're not accountable. /.../ That's not how things are supposed to work. This is not normal.[2]

From Obama's speech you would clearly get the impression that having unelected and yet politicized office holders affecting major political decisions was an exception and an aberration. However, earlier that summer, his own former staffer Ben Rhodes had published his memoirs of his time in the White House. A review thus summarized the position of Rhodes under the Obama presidency:

> By title, he was first Obama's speechwriter for foreign policy and then the deputy national security adviser for communications. Unofficially, he was more than that. Rhodes was the White House official who decided which countries Obama would visit and whom he would meet overseas. He took on special assignments and portfolios, including the secret negotiations that resulted in the establishment of diplomatic relations with Cuba. Above all, Rhodes was the adviser (colleagues like Susan Rice claimed) who had a kind of 'mind meld' with the president – putting Obama's

ideas into words and speeches, deciding on the administration's line about events, sharing ideas with Obama, translating for the bureaucracy how Obama would think.[3]

No one would claim that Rhodes had ever overstepped his authority in the way officials in the White House regularly did under Trump. But the fact that unelected and yet partisan actors have considerable sway over how politics is made is neither new nor exceptional. It is now routine in any advanced democracy, and something that has become more widespread and significant in virtually all polities. This clearly raises issues related to accountability, legitimacy, and trust. From an even more sinister polity, an important account of the 'court' of advisors to Vladimir Putin reminds us that 'in trying to divine the intentions of their leader, his associates effectively materialized their own wishes' (Zygar 2017: 346). Might a democrat have reason to worry?

Rhodes went on from the White House to become a political commentator and to form National Security Action, 'bringing together and mobilizing an unparalleled network of former senior officials and policy experts, academics, and civil society leaders who are dedicated to a progressive vision of American global leadership'.[4] Such moves between government, interest organizations, think tanks, lobbying firms, and other organizations dedicated to political advocacy and policy change are quite typical for actors of Rhodes' ilk. We find them across the rich democracies, in various forms and guises. They are not always very visible and yet they are present in almost all important political and policy-making processes.

This is a book about these political actors, whom I call *policy professionals*. Their numbers extend far beyond the central government offices of powerful nations – and have increased substantially over time. The book is neither an attempt to castigate them as the villains of the modern political drama nor to hail them as the unsung heroes of politics and policy making. Contemporary dramatizations of political life contain plenty of both, as seen on screen in series such as *West Wing, Borgen, In the Thick of It*, and *House of Cards*.

The book is instead the final result of a multidisciplinary research effort to understand the characteristics of this category of political actors. Who are these people, in terms of their modus operandi, backgrounds, driving forces, and careers? What are they doing, why do they do it, and how do they do it? What specific skills do they bring to the political power game and how do they deploy them? And ultimately, what do their actions, their increasing numbers, and their trajectories across organizations imply for our understanding of how democracy works and how political power is wielded?

How should policy professionals be delineated in contrast to other categories of political actors? In this book, the defining characteristics of policy professionals are as follows: they constitute a heterogeneous set of actors who are employed, on a partisan basis, in order to ultimately affect policy. Each of these defining elements needs some elaboration and caveats.

Policy professionals are *employed* and not elected or appointed; they are hired to do policy advocacy and give political advice. This distinguishes them from politicians, who are elected and can be voted out of office. But it also distinguishes them from political actors who are appointed to specific boards or for particular missions; policy professionals work on a regular basis to affect policy and politics. The work of policy professionals can vary in the extent to which it is tied to specific tasks or clients, but it is nevertheless enduring and regular rather than episodic and extraordinary.

Policy professionals are hired on a *partisan* basis, which is not the case for civil servants and other public administrators. They are supposed to share the employing organization's (or client's) values and interests and work for specific causes and orientations. 'Partisan' does not necessarily mean being attached to a specific political party or ideological orientation (although many policy professionals are), but it does mean being committed to promoting causes and values rather than to providing value-neutral expert advice.

Making this distinction does not imply that civil servants and other public administrators never become attached to specific interests and causes, or are never affected by particular ideologies. The recent history of public policy provides plenty of examples of how ostentatiously neutral civil servants or experts harbour certain policy preferences, based on a mixture of academic research and ideological beliefs, and vigorously (and sometimes successfully) pursue these preferences (Babb 2009, Christensen 2017, Fairbrother 2019, Fourcade 2009). However, the basis on which they were hired and the shape of their careers are not tied to a specific partisan orientation in the way they are for policy professionals.

Policy professionals ultimately try to affect *policy*, hence their name. This does not necessarily imply that they are specialists in any particular policy – for example, that they would be experts in social insurance legislation or environment regulation. Some of them certainly are, but their prime expertise – as will be discussed throughout this book – lies in knowing how to influence politics in the broad sense in order to affect policy. Such an intended policy impact does not necessarily mean working to promote policy change; just as often, policy professionals are concerned with trying to stop or slow down policy change. Sometimes the time scale is glacial, such as when think-tankers try to affect the terms of the political debate; sometimes it concerns the here-and-now, such as when a political advisor tries to come up with an immediate solution in a political emergency. And the policies in question do not have to be on a grand scale, affecting the fate of nations and populations; they are more often small and mundane and affect particular constituencies and social groups.

Policy professionals thus constitute a *heterogeneous* set of actors, stretching from political advisors in government offices and parliaments to political support staff in parties, think-tankers, interest organizations' policy experts, and political consultants and lobbyists of various stripes. Although what a political advisor in the government offices does is somewhat different from what a think-tanker, a political director at an interest organization, or a lobbyist does, they share enough characteristics and ways to work to make it fruitful to see them all as part of a broader category of political actors.

The lens chosen for this study is therefore wider than the one previous research in the field has deployed. As will be discussed in Chapter 2, most of this research focuses on specific organizational types or office holders. I argue that looking at policy professionals as a broad, varied, and yet specific category of boundary-spanning political actors – actors that inhabit a particular field in which certain 'rules of the game' apply in the form of explicit and implicit expectations about how to act – will make us see things that organization-specific analyses typically cannot. The policy professionals' careers, networks, and modus operandi span an organizational landscape, and success in their field depends on being able to navigate in this landscape. Organizational and personal commitments matter, as we will find, but ultimately we cannot understand the policy professional phenomenon without taking their whole field and their trajectories in this field into account.

To take the archetypical social democratic welfare state Sweden as an example, the rise of the policy professional category and field has been spectacular in terms of numbers. Even though the appearance of unelected political actors in Sweden is not a recent phenomenon – the first policy professionals had made their entrance already by the early 1950s – they were for a long time only a handful of the people employed as independent experts in the trade unions and business associations, or as special advisors in the government offices. Today, any interest organization that wants to matter employs scores of policy and political specialists, and the number of political appointees in the government offices has gone from 24 in 1975, to 109 in 1995, to close to 200 today (Dahlström 2009, Regeringskansliet 2018). In parliament, the ratio of political secretaries to MPs has gone from roughly 1/10 in the early 1980s to roughly 1/1 today (author's own computations based on parliamentary statistics). Think tanks barely existed in Sweden until the late 1980s; today there are at least a dozen of them that claim some influence on national politics and debate.

Political consultants among PR firms were even later to appear on the scene. In the 1970s there were only two such firms, and it was not until the mid-1990s that they first started to make their impact felt (Tyllström 2013: 14–15). Since then, there has been a virtual explosion of firms that provide political expertise to private business and organized interests. Today, this is an industry with around 1500 employees (Tyllström 2013), at least 200 of which are full-time public affairs consultants, political communication advisors, and others that advise clients on how to proceed politically (Garsten, Rothstein, and Svallfors 2015: Ch. 2).

The total number of policy professional positions in Sweden is now somewhere between 2000 and 3500, depending on how wide the net is cast (Garsten, Rothstein, and Svallfors 2015: Ch. 2). If we include all the people who work as lobbyists at the public affairs departments of large firms, we add several hundred more.

These developments are, of course, not restricted to Sweden and its particular polity. All over the democratic world the number of people who are involved in politics and policy advocacy on a professional and yet partisan basis has grown substantially over the course of the last few decades. Their increasing numbers and more accentuated role in many ways challenge and change politics and policy making as traditionally conceived, and this book is an attempt to show why we should care about these changes.

The aim of this book is not primarily to explain this remarkable rise of policy professionals, but to analyse what their increasing numbers and sophistication mean for democracy and the use of political power. Still, a few words need to be said about the possible driving forces behind their growth in the rich democracies. The literature suggests (at least) three interconnected causes behind this development. One is increasing political complexity. Increased multilevel governance, including various supranational and subnational units, and greater interdependency among policy areas and political outcomes are two of the most important sources of this increased political complexity. But other sources include the multiplying of relevant political actors and stakeholders, and the decline of established forms of collaboration and conflict resolution. All in all, increased political complexity is tackled by bringing in new policy specialists and political advisors to help navigate this complicated landscape.

A second important cause of the expansion of the policy professional field is the intensified mediatization of politics. 'Mediatization' refers to something broader and deeper than simply increased media attention to politics. It includes a far-reaching adaptation of politics to the media logic and to constant media exposure. It means crafting political messages to fit into current modes of mediated communication, and it includes being on constant alert for possible media fallout from decisions and debates. The mass media society of yesteryear at least had things such as newspapers going to the printer and scheduled TV programmes that brought temporary relief from media pressure. In the age of the web and social media, the game has turned into a 24/7 pursuit. Hence, there has been an increasing demand for press secretaries, communication advisers, media specialists, etc., which has further swelled the policy professional ranks.

A third, more contentious, cause of increased policy professionalism is the atrophy of political parties and many civil society organizations. In many places, declining member numbers and ageing member populations is the dominant trend among most political parties and long-standing member organizations. One effect of this is that new political ideas and input have to be sought elsewhere than in ossified member congresses and stifled internal debate. Hence, one attempted solution to this problem is to bring in professionals to generate political ideas and policy proposals that can be of use for the cause.

All three of these tendencies include self-enforcing mechanisms that further increase the demand for policy professionals. Policy professionals not only represent an attempt to tackle increased complexity, they also *contribute* to such complexity through their activities. Policy professionals not only become necessary in a mediatized political environment, they also *drive* the mediatization of political life. And policy professionals not only act as alternative engines for new ideas in parties and organizations, they may also make lay actions to influence such organizations look futile when members are faced with a cadre of highly professional political actors, acting on behalf of the organizational leadership and party leaders.

To further strengthen such self-enforcing tendencies, the very fact that some organizations hire policy professionals makes it imperative for other organizations to hire their own policy professionals so as not to be left behind in the political influence arms race. And the more policy professionals that are hired, the more the supply of their specialized knowledge increases. It is easy to see that it may only be the lack of financial resources that hinders an ever-increasing policy professionalization of the political world.

In this book, the work of policy professionals is approached analytically using a double lens. First, it is analysed as a specific profession with particular acquired skills, which are necessary for successfully accomplishing work tasks and which are in demand across the policy professional labour market. Second, it is studied in relation to issues of political power and democracy, since the work of policy professionals is key to understanding how political influence and democratic accountability function in contemporary advanced democracies.

Hence, in approaching policy professionalism as a specific choice of work and career, which has implications for the functioning of political power and democratic governance, I ask a set of ostensibly naïve questions: *What do policy professionals actually do? How do they do what they do? Why do they do what they do?* These questions relate on the one hand to the skills that policy professionals bring to bear on the political process, and the demand and use for such skills in various organizations in and beyond the policy professional field. On the other hand they relate to the motivations that drive policy professionals in their pursuit. Why are they engaged in political influence work, and why do they prefer to do it in this particular form? The questions relate both to their daily work in a particular organization and to their careers and trajectories across organizations and positions.

This is a different take on the issue than would be typical for a political scientist, who would presumably be most interested in the influence of this group of political actors and ask to what extent this could be measured and evaluated. Their influence would then be compared to that of other elite groups such as capital owners, party leaderships, or university intellectuals. While such a study could certainly be valuable, that is not what this book is. The attempt is not to try to measure the causal impact of policy professionals, or to tell whether they have more or less power than others who are involved in politics and policy making. The question about causal impact is extremely hard to answer in any clear-cut way, since an answer would basically involve re-running history with a different set of actors to see how different processes and outcomes then became.

The purpose of this book is rather to probe the characteristics of this particular set of political actors from a sociological perspective and to ask what their professional skills are made up of and how these skills are deployed in their daily work and throughout their careers. What makes this group of actors particularly intriguing in a sociological perspective is a number of paradoxical traits: they possess skills that are both generic and context-bound; their particular expertise is rare and useful and yet something that cannot be learned in dedicated study programmes; they are both fascinated and repelled by personal or mediatized visibility; their careers span an organizational landscape and yet they face a 'golden cage' problem; they both despise and admire elected politicians; and ultimately they both undermine and invigorate representative democracy. Before the end of this book I hope to put meat on the bones of all these and other fascinating features of policy professionals and their world.

The focus of the book is on the present day rather than on the developmental history of this field of political influence. I will certainly make historical arguments and sometimes ask 'where stuff came from', but the intention is to analyse the policy professional field of action as of today and in the near future.

SWEDEN IN COMPARATIVE PERSPECTIVE

The main setting of the book is Sweden, long regarded as the paradigm of social democratic hegemony and a long-standing corporatist structure for cooperation and conflict resolution. Recently, this political landscape has been swiftly transformed in the direction of a more decentralized, quasi-pluralist, and network-based mode of interest articulation and political advocacy (Lindvall and Rothstein 2006, Lindvall and Sebring 2005, Svallfors 2016). In this transformed institutional setting, the role of various policy professionals has become more accentuated, and their numbers have increased substantially, both inside and outside government (Garsten, Rothstein, and Svallfors 2015).

We may think of Sweden as an interesting test case of how the policy professional field is set up and functions in a post-corporatist country with strong interest organizations and long-standing political parties and divisions. In order to contextualize and contrast findings from Sweden, I therefore bring to bear comparative data from a selection of small European states: the Netherlands, Ireland, and Latvia. I also contrast the findings from the Swedish context to those from Swedish policy professionals working at the European Union (EU) level in Brussels.

The selection of country cases is strategic, focusing on a small selection of comparable country cases that are all democracies, parts of a European frame, similar in size, with proportional electoral systems, and constituted as unitary rather than federal states, but which still represent substantial variety in terms of the political and administrative structure that constitutes the opportunity structure for policy professionals. The case selection therefore includes a long-standing pluralist and yet highly organized setting (the Netherlands), a more personalized political system where local constituencies are key (Ireland), and a more rudimentary and fleeting organizational landscape where the party system, the public administration, and civil society organizations are much more recently formed and substantially weaker than in the long-established democracies of Western Europe (Latvia).

Without trying to write a full comparative institutional analysis of the four countries, a few stylized facts can be brought out to highlight some key similarities and differences among the four countries in how the policy professional organizational field is composed.[5] First, the system of political advisors in government looks strikingly similar across all four countries. In all countries, ministers have a fairly limited number of political advisors (one to three), who are tied to the fate of that particular minister. The same similarity basically applies to the advisor roles in parliaments, where there is a mixture of advisors that are tied to specific MPs and advisors that work for the whole parliamentary group. It seems that in Sweden parliamentary assistants/advisors are least connected to particular MPs, while Ireland displays the strongest links between particular advisors and specific MPs, but differences among countries are not large in this respect.

But once we turn outside politics as narrowly defined, differences in the policy professional field among the four countries become more pronounced. The policy professional capacity among trade unions and major business associations differs substantially across the four countries. Sweden employs scores of policy professionals among such organizations, and a fair deal of what would typically be seen as belonging to the world of think tanks is done in-house in major organizations in Sweden. In the Netherlands, trade unions and employer federations instead jointly host a large research centre, which is geared towards provision of neutral advice and statistics rather than politicized policy professionalism. In Ireland, the policy professional aspects of trade unions and employer federations are lodged in specific think tanks rather than in-house. And in Latvia, the independent analytical capacity of trade unions and business associations is weak almost to the point of non-existence.

The world of think tanks also looks quite different across the four countries. In Sweden, think tanks were virtually non-existent for a long time, no doubt because of the crowded organizational field as described above, and even today most think tanks are financially and organizationally strongly dependent on business associations or trade unions. In the Netherlands, each political party with parliamentary representation hosts its own think tank, which is financially and organizationally separate from the party but provided with a mission to think of long-term issues of a particular ideological orientation. Other think tanks are virtually non-existent. In Ireland, we find a mixture of think tanks attached to trade unions and think tanks financed by philanthropies (of various political and intellectual orientations). In Latvia, there are basically one or two independent think tanks, with a centrist orientation towards the promotion of good governance and fact-based policy making rather than with any specific ideological orientation.

Finally, the world of political PR and lobbying also differs among the four countries. The most crowded lobbying scene is found in the Netherlands, and it is also here that lobbying by private organizations towards government is most long-standing and most accepted as a form of political action. In Sweden, the lobbying/PR business was much later to appear than in the Netherlands, and although it has grown rapidly in the last decades, it is not as widespread nor as legitimate as in the Netherlands. The same lack of legitimacy goes for Ireland, which has a more restricted political lobbying/PR sector than the Netherlands and Sweden, basically restricted to a handful of Dublin firms. And in Latvia, the sector is virtually non-existent; there are only a few small firms in Riga which specialize in political lobbying/PR, and a handful of individual lobbyists.

My aim with the strategic country comparisons is emphatically not to arrive at strong causal statements on the development and strategies of policy professionals, where institutional traits are used to explain similarities and differences across countries. It is rather to contextualize the findings about policy professionals and to arrive at 'a historically informed style of social inquiry that favors properly contextualized generalizations' (Katzenstein 2003: 13). In such a perspective, the facts about the policy professional organizational field are used to interpret and make sense of what we learn from the interviews, and information about certain institutional elements is used to back up interpretations of the findings.

As suggested long ago by Peter Katzenstein, a focus on small states may be highly rewarding in questioning or complementing findings that were based on research on larger countries (Katzenstein 1985, 2003). As he aptly puts it, '[I]f you give a party in the capital, you can easily invite all the important political players. This makes a difference to both politics and policy' (Katzenstein 2003: 11). And it certainly does so for the policy professionals, dependent as they are on their networks and contacts.

The book is mainly based on a large set of semi-structured interviews with policy professionals in Sweden, Ireland, Latvia, and the Netherlands, and with Swedish policy professionals at the EU level in Brussels. Some of the Swedish interviewees have been interviewed twice with about five years in between. These interviews were designed to cover different aspects of the lives and work of policy professionals, and were recorded, transcribed verbatim, and coded for pertinent themes. In addition, my research team quantitatively mapped Swedish policy professionals in 2012 and 2018 in order to study their social composition and careers. All details regarding selection, fieldwork, and coding are found in the Methods Appendix at the end of this book.

WHAT THIS BOOK ADDS

As will be discussed in the next chapter, previous research has had plenty to say about the influence of political and policy experts, about the roles of unelected political actors, and about the importance of political information and know-how. The current book hardly starts from scratch. Yet, something seems amiss. Most research implicitly paints a picture of a political world in which actors and their actions are all part of organizational containers or perhaps silos. We get to know quite a lot about what political advisors do for their principals, or about how think-tankers broker knowledge, or what experts do in policy making. But we are seldom invited to take a broader view, in which we try to understand the systemic consequences of all these various unelected professional political actors and see their activities as spanning a whole organizational landscape.

Although what a political advisor in the government offices does is different from what a think-tanker does, or what a research officer in a trade union does, what they all do is apply expert knowledge in the particular domain of politics. As I will discuss throughout this book, such knowledge can only be acquired on the job; it is highly useful for a variety of organizational types and specific organizations; it can be turned into a marketable commodity; and it is the basis for hierarchy, prestige, and loyalty. For all these reasons, we need a broad inter- and cross-organizational perspective on policy professionals, one that sees them as inhabitants of a social field rather than as purely organizational representatives. Their networks and their careers span organizational borders, and their trajectories in the field shape both them and their organizational destinations.

By analysing policy professionalism and policy professionals as organization-spanning actions and actors, I therefore aim to make one more specific contribution with this book, and two more general ones. The specific contribution is that it will add important aspects to our current understanding of contemporary politics and policy formation. The book will focus on a little-analysed group occupying key positions of influence and power in the political and organizational landscape. It brings in a comparative perspective that will shed light on the role of policy professionals in political and policy processes.

But the book is also intended to provide a more general contribution to normative democratic theory. The rise of the policy professionals – since they are employed to do politics and affect policy rather than being elected to do so – challenges traditional notions of representative democracy (Manin 1997). Legitimation of binding decisions through representation by people elected to office is a cornerstone of democratic theory and practice. The professionalization of politics and policy making that this study taps into challenges this notion in fundamental ways. In the long run, is this dynamic leading towards delegitimization of political power? Or should policy professionals be seen as based in a different form of legitimation – one of professional competence rather than representation (cf. Rothstein 2009)?

Lastly, the book is intended to make a general contribution to the analysis of political power. The work of policy professionals fuses knowledge and power: their field of action includes the mobilization of networks and other social and cognitive resources, and yet it is a highly invisible form of power making (cf. Culpepper 2011, Rhodes 2011). Political power is now restructured in a different mode from what used to be the case in the heyday of mass parties and (quasi-) corporatist decision structures, but social and political science research are still struggling to make sense of the new political power order. In many respects, the current mode of organizing political power increasingly displays curious similarities with pre-democratic modes of organizing it. The how, what, and when of this exercising of power is therefore key to understanding contemporary politics and policy making.

In the chapters that follow, I tell the story about policy professionals from a variety of angles. Chapter 2 provides an overview of the scattered research field to which this book contributes, and discusses key concepts for the analyses.

In Chapter 3, I turn to the action repertoires of policy professionals and discuss what their most important skills are and how they deploy them in the course of action. I highlight the peculiar 'glocal' structure of their skills and actions; they are almost completely context-bound and almost fully generic and context-free at the same time.

Chapter 4 focuses on the motivations of policy professionals. In particular, I ask why they prefer to be involved in politics and policy making in the form they are – why are they neither politicians nor public administrators? I argue that their special relations to issues of visibility and responsibility are what make them prefer politics in the particular policy professional mode.

Chapter 5 (co-written with Niels Selling) turns to the policy professionals' careers. We maintain that the special skill set they acquire and use is very fungible across a broad set of policy professional positions, at the same time as it is mostly limited to these particular positions in the labour market. This creates a certain 'golden cage' problem for policy professionals, one that they try to handle in various ways over the course of their careers.

Chapter 6 (co-written with Anna Tyllström) contains a case study of policy professionals in action, using the peculiar case of the privatization of the Swedish welfare state. We show what a special subset of policy professionals, those employed as lobbyists for the private welfare sector, actually do when they argue their case and serve their principals. Or is it actually the principals serving their policy professionals? As we will find in this chapter, it is far from clear.

The last chapter of the book tries to bring the threads together in an extended discussion of what the policy professional field, and the actions, skills, motivations, and career trajectories that take place in it, actually mean for broader issues of governance, political power, and ultimately democracy in the 21st century. Are policy professionals the gravediggers of representative democracy as we have come to know it, or are they, on the contrary, injecting life and energy into stale structures and procedures? What issues of accountability, representation, and legitimacy do their appearance and proliferation entail? What are their relations to the recent populist and sometimes anti-democratic surge in Europe and across the globe? Should we worry and, if so, what about, exactly?

NOTES

1. https://www.nytimes.com/2018/09/05/opinion/trump-white-house-anonymous
    -resistance.html (accessed 15 January 2019).
2. https://eu.usatoday.com/story/news/politics/elections/2018/09/07/president
    -barack-obamas-speech-transcript-slamming-trump/1225554002/ (accessed 15
    January 2019).
3. New York Review of Books, no. 14, 2018, p. 22, https://www.nybooks.com/
    articles/2018/09/27/ben-rhodes-bliss-dawn-to-be-alive/ (accessed 15 January
    2019).

4. https://nationalsecurityaction.org/ (accessed 15 June 2019).
5. The description of the policy professional organizational field in each country is mostly based on information from the interviews, but also on country descriptions (e.g., Andeweg and Irwin 2014, Auers 2015, Crotty and Schmitt 2014, Hardiman 2012, O'Malley and MacCarthaigh 2011, Tyllström 2013, Ullström 2011).

REFERENCES

Andeweg, Rudy B., and Galen A. Irwin. 2014. *Governance and Politics of the Netherlands*. Basingstoke/New York: Palgrave Macmillan.
Auers, Daunis. 2015. *Comparative Politics and Government of the Baltic States. Estonia, Latvia and Lithuania in the 21st Century*. Basingstoke: Palgrave Macmillan.
Babb, Sarah L. 2009. *Behind the Development Banks: Washington Politics, World Poverty, and the Wealth of Nations*. Chicago, IL/London: University of Chicago Press.
Christensen, Johan. 2017. *The Power of Economists Within the State*. Stanford, CA: Stanford University Press.
Crotty, William J., and David A. Schmitt, eds. 2014. *Ireland and the Politics of Change*. London: Routledge.
Culpepper, Pepper D. 2011. *Quiet Politics and Business Power: Corporate Control in Europe and Japan*. Cambridge: Cambridge University Press.
Dahlström, Carl. 2009. 'Political Appointments in 18 Democracies.' In *QoG Working Paper Series*. Göteborg: Quality of Government Institute.
Fairbrother, Malcolm. 2019. *Free Traders: Elites, Democracy, and the Rise of Globalization in North America*. Oxford: Oxford University Press.
Fourcade, Marion. 2009. *Economists and Societies: Discipline and Profession in the United States, Britain, and France, 1890s to 1990s*, Princeton Studies in Cultural Sociology. Princeton, NJ: Princeton University Press.
Garsten, Christina, Bo Rothstein, and Stefan Svallfors. 2015. *Makt utan mandat. De policyprofessionella i svensk politik*. Stockholm: Dialogos.
Hardiman, Niamh, ed. 2012. *Irish Governance in Crisis*. Manchester: Manchester University Press.
Katzenstein, Peter J. 1985. *Small States in World Markets: Industrial Policy in Europe*. Ithaca, NY/London: Cornell University Press.
Katzenstein, Peter J. 2003. '*Small States* and Small States Revisited.' *New Political Economy* 8 (1): 9–30.
Lindvall, Johannes, and Bo Rothstein. 2006. 'Sweden: The Fall of the Strong State.' *Scandinavian Political Studies* 29 (1): 47–63.
Lindvall, Johannes, and Joakim Sebring. 2005. 'Policy Reform and the Decline of Corporatism in Sweden.' *West European Politics* 28 (5): 1057–74.
Manin, Bernhard. 1997. *The Principles of Representative Government*. New York: Cambridge University Press.
O'Malley, Eoin, and Muiris MacCarthaigh. 2011. *Governing Ireland: From Cabinet Government to Delegated Governance*. Dublin: Institute of Public Administration.
Regeringskansliet. 2018. *Regeringskansliets anställda*. Stockholm, http://httpwww.regeringen.se/regeringskansliet/regeringskansliets-anstallda/ (accessed 1 September 2019).
Rhodes, R.A.W. 2011. *Everyday Life in British Government*. Oxford: Oxford University Press.

Rothstein, Bo. 2009. 'Creating Political Legitimacy: Electoral Democracy versus Quality of Government.' *American Behavioral Scientist* 53 (3): 311–30.
Svallfors, Stefan. 2016. 'Politics as Organized Combat – New Players and New Rules of the Game in Sweden.' *New Political Economy* 21 (6): 505–19.
Tyllström, Anna. 2013. *Legitimacy for Sale. Constructing a Market for PR Consultancy*. Uppsala: Department of Business Studies, Uppsala universitet.
Ullström, Anna. 2011. *Styrning bakom kulisserna. Regeringskansliets politiska staber och regeringens styrningskapacitet*. Stockholm: Stockholm Studies in Politics.
Zygar, Michail. 2017. *All the Kremlin's Men. Inside the Court of Valdimir Putin*. New York: Public Affairs.

2. A research field in the making

In this chapter, I provide the starting point for the analyses that will follow in the empirical chapters. I start by describing the patchy history of the research field and its current scattered status. This is followed by a discussion of the most important theoretical concepts on which the analyses are based. This discussion amounts to a political-sociological perspective in which the key actors are skilled professionals lodged in organizations, working in a specific field, and embedded in institutional settings.

FOUNDATIONS AND FRONTIERS: THE RESEARCH FIELD

What has previous research had to say about policy professionals? Since their appearance is not a recent phenomenon, one could expect that there would now be a substantial corpus of research devoted to these particular political actors. This is not really the case, however. While there are scores of studies on elected politicians, and on public administrators and the civil service, there is far less research on unelected and yet partisan actors. The research is scattered and often takes its starting point in particular types of organizations rather than on a field inhabited by certain actors. It is as if policy professionals have largely managed to fly under the research radar.

Things could have worked out differently. In the US, three foundational texts were published around 1980 that could easily have formed the basis for a comprehensive research programme on policy professionals. Yet, as we will see, this never materialized.

One was political scientist Hugh Heclo's 'Issue Networks and the Executive Establishment' (Heclo 1978). In this text, Heclo identifies a new set of actors in American politics, which indeed he dubs 'policy professionals' but also refers to as 'technopols' or 'policy politicians'. These are political actors who nobody voted for and yet they have substantial political influence. They thrive on complexity because they are the ones who know the nitty-gritty details of policy technicalities and political expediency. Their numbers grow as the decision-making machinery grows in size and complexity, and yet no one outside the corridors of power seems aware of even their existence. They are included in 'issue networks' that span the borders between government and private interests, in which activists for certain issues collaborate and try to affect political decisions.

One struggles in Heclo's text to find any clear definition of what exactly he means by 'policy professionals', 'technopols', or 'policy politicians'. At times, it seems that they include public administrators, political advisors, and interest organization experts (pp. 100ff), but at other times they seem to be something different from the regular public administration (p. 113). Perhaps this vagueness of the category itself is one reason why so little research followed up on Heclo's suggestive argument that the game of political power had been dramatically changed by the appearance of new semi-political players.

Instead, research following from Heclo has focused on the issue networks rather than on the actors involved in them, as I will describe in more detail later. Here, it is asked about the dynamics of such issue networks and what their effects are. The actors themselves are relegated to the shadows (where many of them actually prefer to be – as we will find in this book).

Three years later, fellow political scientist Jack Walker put 'policy communities' on the agenda (Walker 1981). According to Walker, policy communities are characterized by the sustained involvement of what he also calls 'policy professionals', a category that spans the public-private divide and can be found in politics, in the administrative apparatus, in private business, and among media and interest groups. Like Heclo – whom he never cites – Walker focuses on the increasing complexity of politics as a driving force behind the growth of policy communities. The specialized knowledge lodged in the policy communities has become a necessary ingredient in political decision making, making it possible for policy professionals to peddle their favourite solutions to policy problems. He summarizes:

> The political significance of the rise of communities of policy professionals lies not so much in how they affect the daily struggle for bureaucratic authority, but in the subtle and portentous manner in which they are changing the relationship between knowledge and power. (Walker 1981: 93)

Again, this could have been the starting point for sustained research on unelected political actors, but again this did not really happen. Instead, Walker's contribution spawned a cottage industry of studies devoted to the aggregate characteristics and effects of policy communities as collective actors, while the concept of policy professionals remained dormant for a very long time.

And still three years later, yet another American political scientist, John Kingdon, published what would become a classic in policy analysis, *Agendas, Alternatives and Public Policies* (Kingdon 1984 [2011]). In this book, the actors I am interested in are conceptualized as 'policy entrepreneurs'. They are actors that manage to connect the three somewhat independent streams of the policy process – social and political problems, policy solutions, and politics – so as to bring about policy change in the rare moments a 'policy window' opens to allow real change. The policy entrepreneurs are actors with some reputation for being knowledgeable and reliable, who are well connected politically, and who are highly persistent in their undertakings. They are typically not elected politicians but employed professionals with political savvy.

However, the focus in Kingdon's very influential book is mostly on the policy process and the three streams that make up what happens here. Little is said about exactly who these policy entrepreneurs are and exactly how they do what they do in order to bring about policy change. Research following from Kingdon's framework naturally enough followed its leads and tended to focus on the policy processes rather than on the actors involved in them.

In these three foundational texts we find elements with which to conceptualize policy professionals. They work through their networks, they have somewhat fleeting and diffuse mandates for what they do, they have skills regarding both policy making and the political machinery, they are driven by issues and ideas. This could have been a starting point for sustained research about these semi-politicians and how they affect politics and policy making, but this never materialized.

A Scattered Research Field

As a result, the research field to which this book intends to contribute is highly scattered among topics, disciplines, and perspectives. Much of the relevant research focuses on particular types of organizations, networks, or arenas rather than taking a cross-organizational perspective in which the action field and labour market for policy professionals become visible. I will, in a highly stylized fashion, present six partly overlapping areas of research that are highly relevant for my current undertaking.

The first, and the one that most clearly follows the research agenda implied in the foundational texts, is the one concerning *policy/advocacy networks*. This area of research focuses on the networks in which political advocacy towards policy change takes place. These networks are given different names and different emphases by various authors. Some focus on the *issues* that bind such networks together (Knoke et al. 1996), others focus on the forms and directions of *relations* that characterize them (Kriesi 2006). Still others are centred on how loose networks coalesce into advocacy *coalitions* (Sabatier 1988, 1998) or even policy *communities* (Rhodes and Marsh 1992).

Terminology aside, we find differences among the objects of study in the degree of hierarchy and formalization, from open and horizontal network connections to communities that take on traits similar to those of formal organizations, being hierarchical, based on formal membership, and closed to outsiders

(Ahrne 2018, Ahrne and Brunsson 2011). Issue networks are at one end of this spectrum, while policy communities come close to being organizations.

What is common to all these varieties of policy/advocacy networks is that they unite actors who care about specific issues and policies, and who have particular skills in relation to these issues and policies (such as possessing and using specialized relevant knowledge). What they also have in common is that, through their activities, they aim to ultimately affect political decisions and public policies.

These studies have focused primarily on the networks themselves rather than on the actors (Howlett 2002). Sometimes, analysis of the purely formal qualities of networks takes the upper hand, so that both substantive issues and specific actors disappear from view. In contrast, my book puts the actors at the centre and sees their activities in and through networks as means they apply in order to reach their goals. The focus on issues, policies, and the knowledge-power nexus is what I primarily pick from and draw on in this strand of literature.

However, a particular variant of advocacy/policy networks has recently received some research attention that focuses on the actual actors included in the networks. These are composed of 'shadow elites', working as 'flexians' in various 'flexnets' (Wedel 2009, 2014). They are political actors who craft overlapping professional roles to serve their own (and their associates') agendas while purporting to operate in the public interest. Among these players are retired generals who work for defence companies while, at the same time, they sit on government advisory boards that afford them inside access and information. They include 'Key Opinion Leaders' affiliated with top medical schools and journals who appear in influential venues promoting products or treatments and, unbeknownst to their fellow professionals, receive payment or perks from pharmaceutical companies to do so. There are also academic economists who testify before parliamentary and public bodies and the media on economic reform proposals, all the while identifying themselves as academics when they also have contracts with investment banks, as well as ex-leaders on the political world stage who mix philanthropy, business, and public policy in pursuit of their own economic and political agendas. These actors are different from policy professionals in that they typically have multiple and diffuse organizational affiliations, and yet they are similar in that they use networks and information access in order to further their interests.

A second substantial body of literature is focused on *political advisors* in government and in parliament. Here we find research on the roles that political advisors take on in relation to their elected principals, what functions and needs they fill in the political system, and their relations to public administrators and civil servants. Some of the findings in this research, which is mainly based in political science and public administration, can be summarized in a stylized fashion.

Political advisors typically have diffuse mandates and multifaceted roles, which include both political and policy-making tasks. Furthermore, this often entails having a substantial knowledge advantage over elected politicians, since the latter often become very dependent on information provided by their advisors (Askim, Karlsen, and Kolltveit 2017, Blick 2004, Connaughton 2010, 2015, Craft 2016, Eichbaum and Shaw 2008, 2010, Maley 2000, 2011, Yong and Hazell 2014).

In spite of the diffuseness of their mandate, political advisors become necessary adjuncts to leading politicians for two main reasons. They are necessary for handling media and information overload, and for solving steering problems related to the increasing complexity of politics and policy making. At the same time, they contribute to the further mediatization and increasing complexity of politics and policy making (Craft 2016, Dahlström and Pierre 2011).

There are frictions as well as friendly collaboration between political advisors and the civil service (Tiernan 2007). The appearance and growth of political advisors represent, in one sense, a politicizing of the government offices, since there are now scores of political employees involved in policy making. But in another sense this also implies a depoliticization of the civil service, since politically charged tasks are now handled by the advisors rather than permanent civil servants (Christiansen, Niklasson, and Öhberg 2014, Dahlström and Niklasson 2013, Erlandsson 2008).

As shown, existing research has contributed many interesting findings about political advisors in contemporary polities. At the same time, the current state of the art reveals how relatively confining it is to focus only on a particular type of office and organization. While we are presented with scores of findings regarding what political advisors do in their current position, we find almost nothing about where they came from and where they are heading and what this implies for their current job (for important exceptions, see Askim, Karlsen, and Kolltveit 2020, Blach-Ørsten, Mayerhöffer, and Willig 2020). We learn little about how advisors are connected to actors and organizations outside government, through their networks and their careers, and how this affects their opportunities and prospects. As we will find, such questions are fundamental for understanding policy professionalism in the broader sense, and I would argue also for understanding the more restricted category of political advisors.

A third strand in the literature highlights the influence of *policy experts*. In particular, the influence of economists has been highlighted. Academic economists, as representing the most prestigious social science discipline, or economists lodged in government structures, often wield an outsized influence on policy agendas and decisions. As shown by Christensen (2017), Fairbrother (2019), Lindvall (2009), Mandelkern (2019), Mandelkern and Shalev (2010),

Fourcade et al. (2015), and Babb (2009) in a variety of contexts and issues, the influence of academic economists in policy settings is often considerable. They bring technical expertise and a united frame of analysis to bear on issues that are sometimes quite far removed from the domain of economics.[1] At the same time, their influence varies substantially across such contexts and issues. For example, Fairbrother shows that in forging the NAFTA agreement, academic economists were quite influential in Mexico, but much less so in the US where they encountered resistance from the business community (Fairbrother 2019). In a similar vein, Lindvall indicates that the influence of economic experts was 'real but limited' in forging changes in economic policies in a selection of European countries. While economists were highly influential in the selection of policy instruments, they were less so in the change of goals for economic policy away from full employment (Lindvall 2009).

Policy experts are often linked to one another to constitute specific epistemic communities, which share definitions of problems and their possible solutions (Adler and Haas 1992, Haas 1992). Networks of experts and epistemic communities in turn combine to make up the knowledge regimes of different countries, each displaying a particular configuration of public institutions, interest organizations, and political parties (Campbell and Pedersen 2014). Research on epistemic communities or knowledge regimes rarely displays the focus on political actors that characterizes my book; the focus is on the communities and the organizations rather than on the actors and their skills and motivations.

Furthermore, when relating the findings on economic and other experts to the analyses in this book, it should be emphasized that the expertise of policy professionals is of a *different kind* than that of economists and other academic experts. Policy professionals are specialists in the mechanics of politics and policy making rather than in any specific academic discipline. Hence, their expertise is much closer to that of politicians themselves, and more distant from the academic seminar rooms. Yet, what they do have in common with academic economists and other research-based expertise is that they know and can apply things in political life that are typically far beyond the reach of lay actors. And in a similar way to academic experts, they may be less influential in deciding about broad directions and ultimate goals, but highly influential in deciding what means can be most effectively applied to reach such goals.

The research on policy experts is closely connected to the research on *think tanks* and other organizational providers of policy advice and advocacy. The story about the rise and changing contours of the think-tank world is a quite US-centred one. It is focused mainly on the dramatic change from centre-oriented think tanks largely occupied with providing factual information about policy change and impact, to highly combative think tanks preoccupied with advocating for conservative or market-liberal agendas (Barley 2010, Medvetz 2012b, Rich 2004, Saloma 1984, Stone 1996).

Think tanks are typically seen as *mediating* between research on one hand and politics and policy making on the other (Rich 2004, 2011). In this process, they 'translate' research findings into policy ideas and vice versa. But in many cases and respects they are also *competitors* to academic research and may act to marginalize serious scholarship in favour of their own partisan perspectives (Medvetz 2012b). In any case, think-tankers are a particular subgroup among policy professionals in that they marshal research evidence and arguments for their causes at the borderland between academia and politics.

Last but not least, research on *lobbying and communication advice* is highly relevant for the arguments in this book. One strand of research on this topic tries to measure the impact of lobbying, often finding surprisingly small effects of lobbying efforts on outcomes (Baumgartner et al. 2009, for a summary, see Selling 2018: 29–31). Firms and other clients rarely get exactly what they ask for, and there is no straightforward link between spending on lobbying and policy success.

To measure issue-by-issue outcomes, however, is a very restricted way to look at lobbying. More lobbying money goes to supporting political friends than to trying to convince opponents. Lobbying is often a way of subsidizing activities for policy makers who are already convinced of the lobbyist's standpoint, and a way of focusing their attention on issues that are important for clients (Carpenter, Esterling, and Lazer 2004, Hall and Deardorff 2006). Lobbying is therefore best seen as a long-term sustained attempt to build support and coalitions and to weaken opponents (Svallfors and Tyllström 2017).

Many studies analyse the 'revolving door' between lobbying and politics in order to ask what specifically is exchanged at the interface of business and policy making. Some studies, mainly from the US, argue that the most important goods that ex-politicians and ex-staffers trade are network contacts. For example, Blanes i Vidal et al. show that lobbyist ex-staffers from Congress lose on average close to 25 per cent of their income when 'their' representative retires or loses the election, a clear indication that they sell access to the political representatives (Blanes i Vidal, Draca, and Fons-Rosen 2012).

Other studies, however, indicate that while network contacts are certainly valuable, the most important goods that lobbyists trade are knowledge and information about how politics and the broader decision-making apparatus function. Such knowledge is hard to acquire unless one has spent time in politics and policy making, and it expires more slowly than network contacts (Allern 2011, Laurens 2018, Mahoney 2008, Makse 2017, Parker 2009, Tyllström 2019). In Europe, where politics is typically less person-bound than in the US, political skills are probably substantially more important than network contacts in providing leverage for lobbyists.

It is important to note that the revolving door is not a one-way exit. Ex-lobbyists re-enter the world of politics, bringing with them a more communicative and business-oriented way to approach politics and policy making (Tyllström 2019). Hence, the revolving door represents a blurring of institutional spheres, something to which I shall return in subsequent chapters.

* * *

In summary, we can see that there are clearly bits and pieces of research that relate to the broader phenomenon of policy professionalism that this book seeks to tackle. The overview has been stylized and piecemeal, but it indicates that the broad and deep professionalization of politics and policy making that is at the core of this book has certainly received research attention from various disciplines and perspectives. At the same time, research remains scattered and piecemeal rather than encompassing.

FIELDS, POLITICAL SKILLS, AND ORGANIZED POWER: CONCEPTUAL GUIDEPOSTS

In this book I uncover and describe policy professionalism as a *field*. This entails conceptualizing policy professionals as a heterogeneous *boundary-spanning* category, invested with certain *political skills*, which form the basis for a *professionalized* activity within specific *organizations* and certain *institutional* settings. How should we understand these concepts?

Fields and Boundary-spanning Actors

Policy professionals inhabit a field and are lodged within various sorts of organizations. Barley (2010) defines an organizational field as comprising 'a set of organizational populations and the relations that embed members of these populations into a social system or network with a purpose' (Barley 2010: 780). A field may thus be defined as a meso-level social order in which actors interact on the basis of shared understandings about the purposes of the field and their actions within it, about what relations exist to other actors in the field, and about the rules that govern legitimate action in the field (Fligstein and McAdam 2012: 9). As for policy professionals, their field is constituted by the purpose of changing society by political means; it contains multiple relations – to other policy professionals, politicians, and other political actors – and it is governed by a set of explicit and implicit rules (such as acting under the conditions of democratic governance). This focus on meaning, purpose, and understanding is what is essential about the field concept as it is used in this book.[2] It makes it imperative to investigate how the actors view themselves and the meaning of their actions in order to understand what is at stake.

Actors in the field are defined by their relations to one another. As put by White and co-authors, 'fields are supra-organizational transactional linkages that configure the search and regulation systems that govern the interpretation and actions of both organizational and individual participants' (White et al. 2004: 96, quoted in Barley 2010: 798). Such relations contain both collaboration and conflict. In establishing collaboration and conducting conflict, actors use shared meanings and identities strategically to further their own and their organizations' interests in the field (Fligstein and McAdam 2012: 35ff). Here, the 'social skills' of actors in the field are of key importance. 'Social skills' refers to the ability to mobilize other actors for one's own purposes (Fligstein and McAdam 2012: 45ff). Such social skills reside in individuals, but they are inherently based in organizational positions. Acting as part or on behalf of organizations provides actors with a sense of purpose and with key resources for being efficient actors. The lone wolf rarely gets things done; actors need to reach out to other actors in the field in order to achieve their aims. In doing so, the existential aspects of fields and actions within them become paramount. It is only by providing themselves and others with vested meaning that actors in the field can become efficient. Meaninglessness cannot induce action in oneself and others. Hence, policy professionals, like other social actors, need to constantly remind themselves and others about exactly why they do what they do, what meaning is inherent in their field of action.

The field of policy professionals is related to other adjacent fields, such as journalism/media, profit-seeking enterprises, and public administration. In relation to these adjacent fields, and in the internal relations among organizations in their field, policy professionals appear as a boundary-spanning category (Medvetz 2010, 2012a). Their activities, networks, and careers span organizational boundaries both within and outside their field. It is therefore imperative to take an approach that does not remain confined to particular organizations or organizational types when trying to understand policy professionals as a category of actors. Their generic skills and motivations, which can be applied in diverse organizational settings, will only become visible when we apply a broad cross-organizational perspective.

Policy professionals perform a large set of roles and take on a variety of tasks in their capacity as boundary spanners. This variety is displayed not only among different organizational positions that policy professionals hold but also within and among individuals holding similar positions. For example, sociologist Tom Medvetz sees think-tankers as involved in a 'vaudeville act' in which they shift and combine the roles of academic scholar, political aide, entrepreneur, and media specialist, and balance the contradictory imperatives attached to these roles (Medvetz 2010). Similarly, political scientist Bernadette

Connaughton focuses on the very different roles political advisors in government take in relation to their principals, from personal assistants to providers of policy ideas to brokers between politics and administration (Connaughton 2010, see also Craft 2015, Maley 2000). Hence, the roles and boundaries of what policy professionals do are highly mixed and blurred, and individuals may be able to shape their personal roles to a quite significant extent.

Skills and Professionalization

Political skills could be defined as the ability to competently navigate the political system (as broadly conceived) to achieve the desired political results. Such political skills are primarily acquired on the job, although they may be grounded in formal education in relevant subject fields. The empirical analysis will reveal the key ingredients that make up such political skills and how these skills are applied in the course of policy professionals' actions.

It is important to realize that these skills and their application are inherently intertwined with the motivations of individual actors. It would be meaningless to speak of particular skills without taking into account the overarching purpose(s) they serve. Hence, throughout this book I will keep an eye out for the particular motivations that drive policy professionals in their daily endeavours and their careers.

In applying their diverse skills, policy professionals display a professionalized action repertoire, albeit of a somewhat different kind than is found in 'classical' professions. There is of course no formal legitimation required to work as a policy professional, and there are no designated study programmes for becoming one. Yet, at the same time, policy professionals apply expert knowledge in the course of their work – knowledge that is beyond the reach of regular citizens and that takes years to acquire and use in a resourceful manner (Brint 1994). Furthermore, generic academic skills constitute a necessary base for their professional practice. Although it is possible, it is very difficult to acquire such generic skills in places other than universities, and it is rare indeed to find people that have managed to do so.

Furthermore, as we will find, policy professionals are entangled in personalized relationships based on loyalty, trust, and joint ideological standpoints rather than based in neutral and depersonalized expert knowledge. This particular semi-professionalized structure of their work and careers makes them similar to several other professional groups that inhabit insecure and contested occupational niches. By showing how policy professionals are similar to and different from other professional groups, we can more easily locate the specificity of the former. Let me therefore discuss a few of these groups in turn.

One such related group are the 'connective professionals' targeted by public administration scholar Mirko Noordegraaf and his colleagues (Noordegraaf

2007, 2015, Noordegraf, van der Steen, and van Twist 2014). A distinct set of analyses enquire about new forms of professionalism in policy work. In contrast to the 'old' professions, many of the new professions in the public policy field (such as 'programme managers' or 'strategists') tend to merge elements from professional and managerial work and in this way become 'hybrid' professions. Important aspects of their work are the use of network connectivity in order to achieve their aims, and control of the forms in which their work is controlled by others.

Noordegraaf and colleagues focus on public policy professionals who are public administrators rather than on the stratum of partisan professionals that I target. However, their focus on the professional content of the work of policy implementers is highly relevant to my own endeavour. They point out that new forms of policy professionalism are different from the specialized and highly technical skills of old professions in the policy field, and that this new form of professionalism is highly contextual and relations-oriented. As will become obvious, this is something which is characteristic also of the policy professionals in this book.

A second group is the 'itinerant experts' analysed by organizational theorists Stephen Barley and Gideon Kunda (2004). Barley and Kunda focus on temporarily hired skilled professionals who rotate into and out of various organizations and in doing so accumulate marketable experience. They show how emotional labour, such as trust building and skill acquisition and retainment, are key challenges for these skilled professionals as they navigate their labour market. Potential buyers of their skills need to be constantly reassured that they can trust the commitment and expertise of the 'itinerant experts'. And skill acquisition and retainment are constant challenges since they are employed everywhere and nowhere and no one is prepared to take long-term responsibility for their professional development. They have to find ways to update and replenish their skills or they will eventually find themselves out of business. As we will find, such trust building and problems of skill deterioration are also common features in the world of policy professionals.

A third and perhaps somewhat exotic professional group that resembles policy professionals are the wealth managers that sociologist Brooke Harrington put in the focus (Harrington 2016, 2017). These wealth managers have as their professional ethos and goal to protect large fortunes, often in the form of trust funds or foundations. In order to do so, they need not only a healthy dose of detailed technical know-how regarding financial arrangements and legal jurisdictions but also a global outlook since the financial arrangements often straddle locations worldwide. In addition, and fundamentally, they need to build sustained trust with their wealthy clients. To be able to do so, they have to cultivate a certain personal style in how they dress and speak. They have to convey the impression that they are of the same ilk as their clients, that the clients can safely hand over control of their multi-billions in assets and expect their fortune to be safe in the wealth managers' hands. The wealth managers' bonds to their clients therefore take on a strangely personal note in the midst of impersonal financial transactions; they have to get close to the people whose fortunes they guard in order to efficiently pursue their work. In a similar way, as we will find, the policy professionals that are in focus in this book have to get and remain close to their principals if they are to pursue their interests efficiently. The principals have to trust in the loyalty and commitment of the policy professionals, and values have to be shared if unwanted friction is to be avoided.

What makes all these professional groups similar are a few noteworthy characteristics. One is that they all apply expert knowledge to their domain, expert knowledge that is hard to acquire and is beyond the reach of lay actors (cf. Brint 1994). Detailed knowledge about the internal processes of the government offices or about how to design an airport is not widespread. It takes education and long-standing experience to acquire it, and constant updating to keep it fresh and useful.

A second is that this know-how is only partially credentialled and legitimized. If you try to work as a lawyer or a medical doctor without a licence, you will likely be prosecuted. But anyone could in principle work as a policy professional or wealth manager without a formal licence (although no one would be likely to hire you unless you had some form of credentials). There is no formally established knowledge base for the things that 'connective professionals' do, nor is there any designated study programme for becoming a policy professional.[3] The organization that hires a policy professional does not get a licensed practitioner whose skills are formalized and tested and therefore can be trusted.

Instead, trust has to be built on a basis of personalized experience and demonstrated track record. This has to include not only trust in the technical competence of the professionals but in their loyalty to cause and person. Principals have to be convinced that the professionals share their goals and values, and that they are committed to the same cause as their employer. In the case of temporary skilled professionals, these goals, values, and causes can be of a fairly cool and neutral kind, but in the case of wealth managers, trust has to be deeper since the professionals are to be given full view and control over large personal fortunes. This highlights that reputation is fundamental in these semi-professional lines of business. Since trust cannot be based in formal legitimation as in purely professional occupations, a reputation for being honest, reliable, and loyal is absolutely fundamental among semi-professionals. And in the case of policy professionals, the employing organization will only touch those whose commitment and values can be trusted.

Hence, an important difference between policy professionals and other similar semi-professional groups in the labour market is the specific ideological component of work. Policy professionals are drawn into their line of business because of ideological and value commitments, and they have to feel – or at least display – ideological commitment in their daily work. They have to share their employer's (or temporary client's) outlook on society and act accordingly, otherwise they would not be employable or sustainable in their role.

Institutions and Organizations

The rules that guide behaviour in the policy professional (or any other) field can be summarized as institutions. Institutions are 'the formal rules, compliance procedures, and standard operating practices that structure the relationship between individuals in various units of the polity and economy' (Hall 1992: 96). Hence, institutions include both a set of rules and a set of sanctions that may apply if one breaks the rules. Institutions not only include formal rules (such as those embodied in law) but also 'standard operating practices', that is, established organizational routines and practices.

Institutions affect human action in a number of ways: by affecting the distribution of various resources, by creating and maintaining incentives to act in certain ways and not others, and by affecting perceptions and norms about what is accepted and expected behaviour (Mettler and Soss 2004, Steinmo 2008). But institutions never fully determine action, there is always some institutional 'slack' through which actors may circumvent and bend rules, and different institutions may affect action in different and sometimes contradictory directions. This makes individual actors' choices hard to predict and provides sources for gradual change in institutions (Hacker, Pierson, and Thelen 2015, Mahoney and Thelen 2010). However, institutions do have constraining and enabling effects, making some courses of action easier to follow, and others harder.

In the case of policy professionals, the most important institutions that structure their actions are those related to the political system in the broad sense. The electoral system, the intra- and inter-party system, the formal relations between the legislative and executive branches of government, or between the political decision makers and the public administration, are all institutional factors that highly affect what policy professionals can and want to do. These institutions will affect their day-to-day activities as well as their career choices and trajectories, not in any deterministic fashion but by making certain courses of action more feasible and attractive than others. But there are other institutions that are of importance in the policy professional world, such as those structuring the relations between various organized interests (for example, different forms of corporatism), or those that affect the resource distribution among organizations or among individuals (such as the rules included in the tax system).

At the same time, we should remember the boundary-spanning character of policy professionals, which makes this category of political actors less institutionally bound than many other actors in the field. They often work at the interstices of organizations, and without formal credentials, something which makes the institutional 'grip' looser than for many other political actors and professionals. In addition, compared to civil servants and other public administrators, policy professionals are much less formally regulated in their day-to-day activities. One could even say that they are underregulated in the sense that very little is typically said in public law about the position and mandate of even the people who work closely with ministers and civil servants in the government offices (Garsten, Rothstein, and Svallfors 2015: 197–201).

Although they are boundary spanners, policy professionals are – through their employment or contracts – lodged within organizations. Organizations are the constituent units of a field. In contrast to institutions, organizations have an embodied presence (for example, all organizations have an address, and most of them have offices or other premises). Organizations can be defined as decided orders that are closed social relationships, which have borders separating them from other organizations and from the unorganized surroundings. They represent entities where a clear distinction can be made between members and non-members, and which rest on formal authority. Organizations can sanction their members by punishing or excluding them. In contrast to institutions, organizations can be actors, that is, they can decide on a course of action and execute it (Ahrne 2018, Ahrne and Brunsson 2011).

Organizations are linked through networks among their members. Networks consist of ties between nodes (in this case individuals), ties that have a social content (such as friendship or acquaintance). Such networks can be purely inter-organizational, but most often they span organizational borders and therefore act to link organizations through their members (Lin 2001: Ch. 3).

Organizations provide their members with power resources. Few individuals can wield power without an organizational basis; it is through their positions in organizations that they can have an impact (Hacker and Pierson 2010). A typical policy professional would be literally nothing without any form of organizational belonging; there would be no need to take their perspective into account if they had no organization for which they act and speak. At the same time, policy professionals are not merely organizational creatures. Their networks and careers span organizational borders and their being effective actors does not depend solely on any one organization.

The organizations that hire policy professionals have multiplied and are quite varied, but they have one important thing in common. They all aim to somehow affect political decisions and outcomes. This aim could be very narrow and short term, such as when a lobbying organization working on behalf of a paying customer tries to affect the outcome of a specific policy issue, or when a party in government tries to gather enough votes to pass a specific bill. But it could also be expressed as much broader and long-term missions, such as when a think tank tries to affect the general political debate for the coming decade(s).

Regardless of what such organizations try to achieve, policy professionals are essential for reaching these goals, and sometimes even formulating such goals in the first place. Regular rank-and-file members of large-scale organizations typically have little influence on their leadership, but policy professionals typically do have such influence (Skocpol 2003). And small-scale organizations in the field sometimes consist only of policy professionals (and some administrative support staff) and do not have members in any true sense (Papakostas 2011, Walker 2014). The relation between policy professionals and organizations in their field is therefore one of mutual dependence and benefit.

* * *

What this adds up to is a particular perspective on political action and order. This perspective has no need for fictions such as the 'parliamentary steering chain' that is often found in political science textbooks (akin to the fiction of the fully competitive market used to drill Econ 101 students). It is a perspective that sees professionals, working in a field and lodged in intra- and inter-organizational settings, as prime movers in politics and policy making. Some of these professionals – the ones I focus on in this book – are hired on a partisan basis, and their expertise is primarily found in what they know about the functioning of politics itself. It is to their particular form of professionalism that this book is devoted.

NOTES

1. A striking Swedish example is the 'Lindbeck Commission' (nicknamed after its chair, economics professor Assar Lindbeck) from the early 1990s. Its final report pronounced on everything from the training of journalists to the ideal number of MPs and homework for schoolchildren, seemingly without much regard for the limitations of specific disciplinary perspectives (Lindbeck et al. 1994).
2. Many fellow sociologists tend to believe that to use the field concept is to align oneself to Pierre Bourdieu's sociological perspective. However, the field concept is used widely in the sociology of organizations literature, with or without any connection to Bourdieu's specific take on sociology. In this book, I refrain from entering into a discussion of the Bourdieusian conceptual framework. It entails

too many assumptions that I do not share, and any discussion of these would risk sidetracking the analysis.

3. The closest thing to a designated study programme for becoming a policy professional is probably the Philosophy, Politics, and Economics (PPE) programmes of many universities. However, the PPE programmes are targeted towards a broader labour market than the policy professional one, and no licence for any specific occupation results from taking the programme.

REFERENCES

Adler, E., and P.M. Haas. 1992. 'Epistemic Communities, World-Order, and the Creation of a Reflective Research-Program – Conclusion.' *International Organization* 46 (1): 367–90.

Ahrne, Göran. 2018. 'The Organization of Action.' In *Concepts in Action*, edited by Håkon Leiulfsrud and Peter Sohlberg, pp. 172–88. Leiden: Brill.

Ahrne, Göran, and Nils Brunsson. 2011. 'Organizations Outside Organizations: The Significance of Partial Organization.' *Organization* 18 (1): 83–104.

Allern, Sigurd. 2011. 'PR, Politics and Democracy.' *Central European Journal of Communication* 12 (1): 125–39.

Askim, Jostein, Rune Karlsen, and Kristoffer Kolltveit. 2017. 'Political Appointees in Executive Government: Exploring and Explaining Roles Using a Large-N Survey in Norway.' *Public Administration* 95 (2): 342–58.

Askim, Jostein, Rune Karlsen, and Kristoffer Kolltveit. 2020. 'Public Office as a Stepping-Stone? Investigating the Careers of Ministerial Advisors.' *Political Studies Review*, doi: https://doi.org/10.1177%2F1478929920906991.

Babb, Sarah L. 2009. *Behind the Development Banks: Washington Politics, World Poverty, and the Wealth of Nations*. Chicago, IL/London: University of Chicago Press.

Barley, Stephen. 2010. 'Building an Institutional Field to Corral a Government: A Case to Set an Agenda for Organization Studies.' *Organization Studies* 31: 777–805.

Barley, Stephen, and Gideon Kunda. 2004. *Gurus, Hired Guns, and Warm Bodies: Itinerant Experts in a Knowledge Economy*. Princeton, NJ: Princeton University Press.

Baumgartner, Frank R., Jeffrey M. Berry, Marie Hojnacki, David C. Kimball, and Beth L. Leech. 2009. *Lobbying and Policy Change: Who Wins, Who Loses, and Why*. Chicago, IL: University of Chicago Press.

Blach-Ørsten, Mark, Eva Mayerhöffer, and Ida Willig. 2020. 'From Government Office to Private PR: Career Patterns of Special Ministerial Advisers and the Privatization of Politics.' *International Journal of Press/Politics* 25 (2): 301–19.

Blanes i Vidal, Jordi, Mirco Draca, and Christian Fons-Rosen. 2012. 'Revolving Door Lobbyists.' *American Economic Review* 102 (7): 3731–48.

Blick, Andrew. 2004. *People Who Live in the Dark*. London: Politico's.

Brint, Steven. 1994. *In an Age of Experts. The Changing Role of Professionals in Politics and Public Life*. Princeton, NJ: Princeton University Press.

Campbell, John L., and Ove K. Pedersen. 2014. *The National Origins of Policy Ideas: Knowledge Regimes in the United States, France, Germany and Denmark*. Princeton, NJ: Princeton University Press.

Carpenter, Daniel, Kevin Esterling, and David Lazer. 2004. 'Friends, Brokers and Transitivity: Who Informs Whom in Washington Politics?' *Journal of Politics* 66 (1): 224–46.

Christensen, Johan. 2017. *The Power of Economists Within the State.* Stanford, CA: Stanford University Press.

Christiansen, Peter Munk, Birgitta Niklasson, and Patrik Öhberg. 2014. 'Politicization One Way or Another: The Organisation of Political Advice and of Civil Servants in Denmark and Sweden.' Working Paper, Department of Political Science, Göteborg University.

Connaughton, Bernadette. 2010. 'Glorified Gofers, Policy Experts or Good Generalists: A Classification of the Roles of the Irish Ministerial Adviser.' *Irish Political Studies* 25 (3): 347–69.

Connaughton, Bernadette. 2015. 'Navigating the Borderlines of Politics and Administration: Reflections on the Role of Ministerial Advisers.' *International Journal of Public Administration* 38 (1): 37–45.

Craft, Jonathan. 2015. 'Conceptualizing the Policy Work of Partisan Advisers.' *Policy Sciences* 48 (2): 135–58.

Craft, Jonathan. 2016. *Backrooms and Beyond. Partisan Advisers and the Politics of Policy Work in Canada.* Toronto: University of Toronto Press.

Dahlström, Carl, and Birgitta Niklasson. 2013. 'The Politics of Politicization in Sweden.' *Public Administration* 9 (4): 891–907.

Dahlström, Carl, and Jon Pierre. 2011. 'Steering the Swedish State. Politicization as a Coordinating Strategy.' In *Steering from the Centre: Strengthening Political Control in Western Democracies*, edited by Carl Dahlström, B. Guy Peters, and Jon Pierre, pp. 193–211. Toronto University of Toronto Press.

Eichbaum, Chris, and Richard Shaw. 2008. 'Revisiting Politicization: Political Advisors and Public Servants in Westminster Systems.' *Governance* 21 (3): 337–63.

Eichbaum, Chris, and Richard Shaw, eds. 2010. *Partisan Appointees and Public Servants: An International Analysis of the Role of the Political Adviser.* Cheltenham, UK and Northampton, MA, USA: Edward Elgar Publishing.

Erlandsson, Magnus. 2008. 'Regeringskansliet och medierna: Den politiska exekutivens resurser och strategier för att hantera och styra massmedia.' *Statsvetenskaplig tidskrift* 110 (4): 335–49.

Fairbrother, Malcolm. 2019. *Free Traders: Elites, Democracy, and the Rise of Globalization in North America.* Oxford: Oxford University Press.

Fligstein, Neil, and Doug McAdam. 2012. *A Theory of Fields.* Oxford: Oxford University Press.

Fourcade, Marion, Etienne Ollion, and Yann Algan. 2015. 'The Superiority of Economists.' *Journal of Economic Perspectives* 29 (1): 89–114.

Garsten, Christina, Bo Rothstein, and Stefan Svallfors. 2015. *Makt utan mandat. De policyprofessionella i svensk politik.* Stockholm: Dialogos.

Haas, P.M. 1992. 'Epistemic Communities and International-Policy Coordination – Introduction.' *International Organization* 46 (1): 1–35.

Hacker, Jacob S., and Paul Pierson. 2010. *Winner-Take-All Politics: How Washington Made the Rich Richer – and Turned Its Back on the Middle Class.* New York: Simon & Schuster.

Hacker, Jacob S., Paul Pierson, and Kathleen Thelen. 2015. 'Drift and Conversion: Hidden Faces of Institutional Change.' In *Advances in Comparative-Historical Analysis*, edited by James Mahoney and Kathleen Thelen, pp. 180–208. Cambridge: Cambridge University Press.

Hall, Peter A. 1992. 'The Movement from Keynesianism to Monetarism: Institutional Analysis and British Economic Policy in the 1970s.' In *Structuring Politics. Historical Institutionalism in Comparative Analyses*, edited by Sven Steinmo, Kathleen Thelen, and Frank Longstreth, pp. 90–113. Cambridge: Cambridge University Press.

Hall, Richard L., and Alan V. Deardorff. 2006. 'Lobbying as Legislative Subsidy.' *American Political Science Review* 100 (1): 69–84.

Harrington, Brooke. 2016. *Capital Without Borders: Wealth Managers and the One Percent*. Cambridge, MA: Harvard University Press.

Harrington, Brooke. 2017. 'Habitus and the Labor of Representation among Elite Professionals.' *Journal of Professions and Organization* 4 (3): 282–301.

Heclo, Hugh. 1978. 'Issue Networks and the Political Establishment.' In *The New American Political System*, edited by Anthony King, pp. 87–124. Washington, DC: The American Enterprise Institute.

Howlett, Michael. 2002. 'Do Networks Matter? Linking Policy Network Structure to Policy Outcomes: Evidence from Four Canadian Policy Sectors 1990–2000.' *Canadian Journal of Political Science* 35 (2): 235–67.

Kingdon, John W. 1984. *Agendas, Alternatives, and Public Policies*. Updated 2nd edn in 2011. *Longman Classics in Political Science*. Boston: Longman.

Knoke, David, Franz Urban Pappi, Jeffrey Broadbent, and Yutaka Tsujinaka. 1996. *Comparing Policy Networks. Labor Politics in the US, Germany, and Japan*. Cambridge: Cambridge University Press.

Kriesi, Hanspeter. 2006. 'Comparative Analysis of Policy Networks in Western Europe.' *Journal of European Public Policy* 13 (3): 341–61.

Laurens, Sylvain. 2018. *Lobbyists and Bureaucrats in Brussels. Capitalism's Brokers*. New York: Routledge.

Lin, Nan. 2001. *Social Capital. A Theory of Social Structure and Action*. Cambridge: Cambridge University Press.

Lindbeck, Assar, Per Molander, Torsten Persson et al. 1994. *Turning Sweden Around* (Swedish original: *Nya villkor för ekonomi och politik. SOU 1993:16*). Cambridge, MA: MIT Press.

Lindvall, Johannes. 2009. 'The Real But Limited Influence of Expert Ideas.' *World Politics* 61 (4): 703–30.

Mahoney, Christine. 2008. *Brussels versus the Beltway. Advocacy in the United States and the European Union*. Washington, DC: Georgetown University Press.

Mahoney, James, and Kathleen Thelen. 2010. 'A Theory of Gradual Institutional Change.' In *Explaining Institutional Change: Ambiguity, Agency, and Power*, edited by James Mahoney and Kathleen Thelen, pp. 1–37. New York: Cambridge University Press.

Makse, Todd. 2017. 'A Very Particular Set of Skills: Former Legislator Traits and Revolving Doot Lobbying in Congress.' *American Political Research* 45 (5): 866–86.

Maley, Maria. 2000. 'Conceptualising Advisers' Policy Work: The Distinctive Policy Roles of Ministerial Advisers in the Keating Government, 1991–96.' *Australian Journal of Political Science* 35 (3): 449–70.

Maley, Maria. 2011. 'Strategic Links in a Cut-throat World: Rethinking the Role and Relationships of Australian Ministerial Staff.' *Public Administration* 89 (4): 1469–88.

Mandelkern, Ronen. 2019. 'Neoliberal Ideas of Government and the Political Empowerment of Economists in Advanced Nation-States: The Case of Israel.' *Socio-Economic Review*, https://doi.org/10.1093/ser/mwz029.

Mandelkern, Ronen, and Michael Shalev. 2010. 'Power and the Ascendancy of New Economic Policy Ideas: Lessons from the 1980s Crisis in Israel.' *World Politics* 62 (3): 459–95.

Medvetz, Thomas. 2010. '"Public Policy is Like Having a Vaudeville Act": Languages of Duty and Difference among Think Tank-Affiliated Policy Experts.' *Qualitative Sociology* 33: 549–62.

Medvetz, Thomas. 2012a. 'Murky Power: "Think Tanks" as Boundary Organizations.' *Research in the Sociology of Organizations* 34: 113–33.

Medvetz, Thomas. 2012b. *Think Tanks in America*. Chicago, IL: University of Chicago Press.

Mettler, Susanne, and Joe Soss. 2004. 'The Consequences of Public Policy for Democratic Citizenship: Bridging Policy Studies and Mass Politics.' *Perspectives on Politics* 2 (1): 55–73.

Noordegraaf, Mirko. 2007. 'From "Pure" to "Hybrid" Professionalism in Ambiguous Public Domains.' *Administration & Society* 39 (6): 761–85.

Noordegraaf, Mirko. 2015. 'Hybrid Professionalism and Beyond: (New) Forms of Public Professionalism in Changing Organizational and Societal Contexts.' *Journal of Professions and Organization* 2 (2): 187–206.

Noordegraaf, Mirko, Martijn van der Steen, and Mark van Twist. 2014. 'Fragmented or Connective Professionalism? Strategies for Professionalizing the Work of Strategists and Other (Organizational) Professionals.' *Public Administration* 92 (1): 21–38.

Papakostas, Apostolis. 2011. 'More Organization with Fewer People.' In *Nordic Civil Society at a Cross-roads: Transforming the Popular Movement Tradition*, edited by Filip Wijkström and Annette Zimmer, pp. 73–107. Baden-Baden: Nomos.

Parker, Glenn R. 2009. *Capitol Investments: The Marketability of Political Skills*. Ann Arbor, MI: University of Michigan Press.

Rhodes, R.A.W., and David Marsh. 1992. 'New Directions in the Study of Policy Networks.' *European Journal of Political Research* 21 (3): 181–205.

Rich, Andrew. 2004. *Think Tanks, Public Policy, and the Politics of Expertise*. Cambridge: Cambridge University Press.

Rich, Andrew. 2011. 'Ideas, Expertise, and Think Tanks.' In *Ideas and Politics in Political Science Research*, edited by Daniel Béland and Robert Henry Cox, pp. 191–208. Oxford: Oxford University Press.

Sabatier, Paul A. 1988. 'An Advocacy Coalition Framework of Policy Change and the Role of Policy-Oriented Learning Therein.' *Policy Sciences* 21 (2–3): 129–68.

Sabatier, Paul A. 1998. 'The Advocacy Coalition Framework: Revisions and Relevance for Europe.' *Journal of European Public Policy* 5 (1): 98–130.

Saloma, John S. 1984. *Ominous Politics. The New Conservative Labyrinth*. New York: Hill and Wang.

Selling, Niels. 2018. *Unity or Fracture? Explaining Political Preference Formation among Large American, Bristish, and German Firms*. Firenze: European University Institute.

Skocpol, Theda. 2003. *Diminished Democracy: From Membership to Management in American Civic Life*. Norman, OK: University of Oklahoma Press.

Steinmo, Sven. 2008. 'Historical Institutionalism.' In *Approaches in the Social Sciences*, edited by Donatella Keating and Michael Della Porta, pp. 113–38. Cambridge: Cambridge University Press.

Stone, Diane. 1996. *Capturing the Political Imagination: Think Tanks and the Policy Process*. London: Frank Cass.

Svallfors, Stefan, and Anna Tyllström. 2017. 'Resilient Privatization: The Puzzling Case of For-Profit Welfare Providers in Sweden.' *Socio-Economic Review* 17 (3): 745–65.

Tiernan, Anne. 2007. *Power Without Responsibility: Ministerial Staffers in Australian Governments from Whitlam to Howard*. Sydney: University of New South Wales Press.

Tyllström, Anna. 2019. 'More Than a Revolving Door: Corporate lobbying and the Socialization of Institutional Carriers.' *Organization Studies*, https://doi.org/10.1177/0170840619848014.

Walker, Edward T. 2014. *Grassroots for Hire. Public Affairs Consultants in American Democracy*. New York: Cambridge University Press.

Walker, Jack L. 1981. 'The Diffusion of Knowledge, Policy Communities and Agenda Setting: The Relationship of Knowledge and Power.' In *New Strategic Perspectives on Social Policy*, edited by John E. Tropman, Milan J. Dluhy, and Roger M. Lind, pp. 75–96. New York: Pergamon Press.

Wedel, Janine R. 2009. *Shadow Elite. How the World's New Power Brokers Undermine Democracy, Government, and the Free Market*. New York: Basic Books.

Wedel, Janine R. 2014. *Unaccountable: How Elite Power Brokers Corrupt Our Finances, Freedom, and Security*. New York: Pegasus Press.

White, Douglas R., Jason Owen-Smith, James Moody, and Walter W. Powell. 2004. 'Networks, Fields and Organizations: Micro-Dynamics, Scale and Cohesive Embeddings.' *Computational & Mathematical Organization Theory* 10 (1): 95–117.

Yong, Ben, and Robert Hazell. 2014. *Special Advisers: Who They Are, What They Do and Why They Matter*. Oxford: Hart.

3. Glocal political action: generic skills, local application

I do understand power, whatever else may be said about me.
I know where to look for it, and how to use it.
(Lyndon Baines Johnson)

When I interview policy professionals in different offices and countries, sometimes interviewees ask me about how it works in other places. This is often followed by comments along the lines of 'I think we are quite different from how they work in other places,' or 'I think my outlook/background/experience is quite special.' If this question comes early in the interview I usually refrain from making clear just how similar they are to other policy professionals in other places. I do not want to ruin a good interview atmosphere, and allowing the interviewee to hang on to the feeling of being in some sense special makes them more prone to talk.

But as I will argue in this chapter, the skills that policy professionals use in their work are actually of a quite generic kind, applicable in very similar formats across organizational and national boundaries. At the same time, policy professionals are extremely locally dependent in what they do. They need particularized knowledge and local network contacts to be efficient in their role, and very little of what they know is immediately applicable in different settings. This somewhat paradoxical 'glocal' (global/local) nature of their work and their skills is something we will delve into further in this chapter, to try to pinpoint what policy professional skills consist of and how they are applied.

CONTESTED SPACE

To begin, one should note that the space in which policy professionals can apply their skills and build their networks is circumscribed but has diffuse borders. This is a clear instance where the boundary-spanning characteristics of policy professionals come into focus, and one where the policy professionals' social skills become important in carving out and maintaining their space for action. In relation to the elected or appointed leadership, be it in political parties or interest organizations, it is often far from clear where the responsibilities of policy professionals start and where they end. This makes it less than clear-cut to decide whether and when policy professionals transgress the legitimate boundaries of their mandate. These boundaries are fleeting and constantly under implicit negotiation and change. Where they are drawn clearly affects how much room for manoeuvre there is for policy professionals in their organizational settings, and ultimately how much they can affect the course of action.

Policy professionals are typically quite aware that their boundaries for action are diffuse and fleeting and have to be constantly renegotiated in the quick pace of their daily work. A political advisor in a Dutch government department put a reflexive spin on the question of where the boundaries of his work are drawn:

> I'm doing other people's job because otherwise it's not fixed for [the minister]. So I mean, if he for example needs to give a speech but there's not a good speech, then I'm rewriting the speech. It's not my job but I'm doing it. Maybe it is my job, but formally it's someone else's job. But I don't think that's your real question. I think your question is if I'm crossing boundaries of my responsibilities.
> *Yes, towards what really should be completely on the minister's table.*
> There is of course like … this is my table, this is his table, there is a grey line here and sometimes you cross it and then you think, 'I should have discussed this before I did it.' It's inevitable. Because you want to keep things away from him, and that's not black and white.

In this 'keeping things away from him', the policy professional displays loyalty to the principal, in this case the minister. The principal has limited time and attention, and filtering which and what kinds of issues should be allowed to bother him/her is being a loyal employee. However, at the same time, the advisor carves out more space for his own actions. To decide what goes to the minister and what can be decided by oneself is to engage in substantial power brokering.

The boundaries are just as fleeting in relation to MPs as they are towards government ministers. The implicitness of the division of labour between the MP and the advisor comes out distinctively in a young Latvian political advisor's pondering over the boundaries to the MP's role:

> *Do you ever think it's hard to define the border between what you should do and what the MP should do, or is there some kind of border?*
> I never thought about it actually. Because sometimes I'm doing what the MP should do actually, yes. It's true! But we have never had conflicts about it, so I'm just informing them that I'm doing something and actually I also like to sometimes … sometimes I come to the discussions of the MPs when my MP cannot come. Then I come and represent him. So actually it is the work of MPs.

As shown by these two quotations, being a policy professional is indeed a very diffuse role, which can comprise different content depending on how the incumbents choose to view their mission. For most policy professionals this role diffuseness is palpable. Some of them even see this as a great advantage. A political secretary in the Swedish parliament claims that the role of a political secretary can be shaped 'exactly as I want. I can quite simply make that role very perfect for me.'

Others are more uncertain about the space and mandate they really have in relation to the elected politicians. There are limits to the mandate, but no one seems sure about exactly what those limits are, as put by this political advisor in the Swedish government offices:

> I have never had a presentation about where that boundary should be. So I don't know at all where that boundary is. You see, I'm here at [the minister's] good understanding and ... goodwill and [the minister] may fire me tomorrow if they want to. I don't know ... I don't think that the boundary ... It is very unclear where that boundary would be.

From the other side of the boundary it is also the case that the boundaries are anything but obvious and self-evident. A Swedish ex-minister with a far-ranging experience of government and cabinet work first claims that the boundary is obvious and clear-cut. Political advisors should simply not be part of policy making. They should be kept 'away from politics, from the policy development' because their involvement would 'choke the line of command' between the minister and the civil servants. And this is how it worked during this minister's term of office. But only 14 minutes later in the interview, the boundary is no longer so clear-cut. Now the ex-minister claims that the 'underlings should take their own initiatives and be forward and make suggestions', as might be shown by 'taking part in the policy development just like everybody else'. That a person with such a long and broad experience from the inner rooms of political power speaks in such a contradictory way must be taken as strong support for the argument that the space for action of the political employees is truly fleeting and diffuse.

One important aspect of the space for policy professionals is that many of them act as gatekeepers, filtering what issues and which information should be allowed to disturb the leading politician or the organizational leadership. After all, the reason why many policy professionals were employed in the first place was to help government ministers and elected or appointed organization leaders cope with the unrelenting flood of information and requests. Acting as a gatekeeper and filter is therefore very much part of the job description. But at the same time, this provides many policy professionals with discretionary and discreet power, since they are the ones who decide what leaders get to see and hence decide about.

This could easily be portrayed as a usurpation of power by the unelected policy professionals. This is rarely really the case, however. The main reason for this is that the elected leadership and policy professionals most often work together as a team, where boundaries are fleeting but underlying values and interests are shared. Policy professionals seek to attach themselves to people, causes, and organizations with which they feel a strong affinity, and hiring organizations want to be sure that the policy professionals they hire share the organization's basic values and understandings. The potential democratic problem lies elsewhere, namely, in a growing distance between rank-and-file members and the organizational leadership. If information is filtered and access restricted, the opportunities for ordinary party or organiza-tional members to exert any real influence on their leadership become small indeed. This leadership vs. membership problem was certainly not instigated by policy professionals – it was observed already in the early days of dem-ocratic organization (Michels 1911 [1962]) – but it has been aggravated by the appearance of a large stratum of professionals that act as gatekeepers and filters between rank-and-file members and their elected leadership.

Even if relations between elected representatives and policy professionals are often harmonious and mutually beneficent, there are instances of trans-gressing of boundaries. Sometimes policy professionals take on clearly pater-nalistic roles vis-à-vis their principals, where the helper suddenly becomes the patron. A Swedish political advisor in the European Parliament describes the relation to the elected MEP:

> Having pedagogical responsibility means presenting this to Maria [fictious name] in a way so that [she] feels part of the decisions we make. /.../ That is why we write PMs and also go through all our work here with [her] and so on. So we talk and discuss and all that. So that [she] feels that [she] is part of it. So that we do not run [her] over and say 'yes we do this because of this and that' and so on, but in a way so that when [she] does something [she] knows why and we have discussed it beforehand.

In this quote, the role division between principal and agent seems to have been turned almost on its head, with the employed advisor staking out what course to follow and then educating the elected representative about how things should work, albeit in a way so that 'we do not run her over'. Situations such as these are most likely to occur when the elected representative is inexperienced and/or less apt in the role. Then a power vacuum appears which some policy professionals are happy to fill.

On the other hand, transgressing boundaries can be highly risky for the policy professional if and when the elected leadership decides that an unacceptable transgression has taken place. An Irish think-tanker on the way out of office describes how the separation began:

> So I gave political views on things that weren't the organization's political view. I was just making my personal point. So there was a major issue around that and they were very concerned and upset by it. I hadn't fully taken on board 'ok, I'm not an individual now and I cannot comment as I want.'
> *How did that play out? Did they call you in for a meeting?*
> Yes, yes, they called me in for a meeting and said 'you just cannot do this.' Strong words were had.

What emerges clearly from quotes such as these two is that the relative power balance and space for action of policy professionals is very much affected by how skilled and experienced their elected principal is. A political advisor in the Dutch government reflects on a how a recent, unexpected, and big election victory brought many inexperienced MPs into the parliamentary group and how that has changed the work of the advisor:

> *Do you ever find it problematic to define the boundary of what you should do and what your MP should do, and is there such a boundary at all?*
> Yes, and it has really changed during the last couple of months and you can see that for some new MPs it's really necessary to spell everything [out] before they go to debate or to say sometimes very clearly 'no, this is not a good idea.' Which is really weird because I'm an advisor and they should know what direction we're going. But sometimes they just don't know. It's very nice to work for an MP who has a very clear vision of which direction we're going, but when they don't and you start to get into their space, obviously. That's sometimes difficult and it's not always clear what the boundaries are.

Even if this situation is presented as problematic in this quote, other parts of the interview make clear how much this advisor enjoys influencing the direction of the party. Hence, there is clear ambivalence among many political advisors in relation to the limits of their space of action. On the one hand, they enjoy working for a strong political leader who is sure about direction and can effect real change. On the other hand, weaker and less experienced elected leaders create more space for the policy professional to exert personal influence and apply their specific skills in politics and policy making.

It is worth emphasizing that although the problems of contested space and boundaries for action become particularly acute for policy professionals who work closely with politicians, they are far from absent anywhere in the policy professional field. They emerge in relation to any principal and any agent in the field and are typically negotiated and solved in the flow of events and in the course of swift action.

KNOWING THE GAME

Using experts of various kinds in public policy making is neither new nor particularly controversial in itself. We want engineers to make sure that bridges and buildings are built according to standards and do not fall apart, and we want doctors and lawyers to make sure that treatments are adequate and laws not contradictory. We ask economists about the effect of changes in the interest rates and scientists about how emissions of carbon dioxide affect the climate. There are certainly disagreements as to what exactly are suitable matters for experts to decide on and what is best left to our political representatives. But the actual need for subject matter knowledge is hardly in dispute.

When it comes to the expertise of policy professionals, though, things are more complicated and controversial. Their expert skills lie not in any particular subject matter but in politics itself. It is through their knowledge of the political system that they serve their employers with essential expertise. In this case, it is far from self-evident that the expertise serves a wider public interest. Depending on who holds such expertise and how they use it, it might even undermine democratic procedures and legitimacy. Such expertise is also a manifestation of political inequality in itself. We do not ask that everyone should be a surgeon or a mechanical engineer, but democracy is built on political equality, and the existence of wide disparities in political expertise therefore becomes a democratic problem in and of itself.

But what, more specifically, does the expertise of policy professionals consist of? What are the skills that they put to use in their daily work? Based on analyses of the interviews, they can be summarized under three headings: *framing problems*, *knowing the game*, and *accessing information*.

Framing problems is about describing contemporary society using descriptions grounded in facts and science but presented from an angle that benefits the values and groups that one represents and suggesting possible policy solutions.

The systematic marshalling and presenting of new evidence is an important power resource in the craftsmanship of the policy professional. Research is engaged and new facts and standpoints are produced. This has to be done in a reliable and scientific way to increase trustworthiness, but it is all done in order to advance the conditions for the groups and interests that one is employed to promote.

A trade union research officer in Sweden explains how it works:

> I really try to present it in as nuanced a way as possible. But then of course I have a real interest in focusing on research and evidence-based knowledge that speaks for our perspective. But I also try to focus on things that speak against us, our opponents' best arguments. Because I also think that our representatives gain from

learning about this and thinking about it. Then they can sharpen their own argumentation. /.../ If I had worked as a speechwriter or as an information officer close to the representative, then my task would have been to spin that information. But that is not my task, as a research officer, to spin it; that is the task of the speechwriters. /.../ My report should be nuanced so they can pick and choose from it. If I had already put a spin on it, then there is a risk that it would be very biased. And then our representatives would maybe lose credibility in the eyes of the public. Therefore it is important that my report is very similar to a sort of research overview.

A couple of things are noteworthy about the quote. The first is that the interviewee sees the role as one akin to that of a researcher. But it is not truth-seeking in a dispassionate way, it is truth-seeking in the service of particular values and causes, in this case those of the Swedish labour movement and the working class. In this interest-based truth-seeking, it is important not to lose credibility, one's own or that of the organization one works for. So everything has to be fact-based in order to be efficient. But of course the framing and selection of data matter, and the ultimate aim is not to present an impartial investigation but to win the argument.

Policy professionals, regardless of context, tend to present the framing of problems as something of a battle, where facts and arguments are the weapon and shield against similarly equipped opponents. This is important, first, to benefit the organization one works for. Facts that turn out to be wrong or severely biased harm the organization; arguments that are correct and based on thorough research help it. But it is also important for the individual policy professional. If exposed as sloppy or untrustworthy, policy professionals undermine their labour market value, which would be detrimental to their careers. The credibility that an academic degree or long-standing professional experience bestows can be easily undermined by presenting shoddy work or false facts.

The second noteworthy thing is that this research officer clearly sees the role as something different from that of a communicator. The task is emphatically not to 'put a spin' on facts but to provide as good a factual base as possible. But in most cases the line between research and communication is less clear-cut than it is as presented by this interviewee. Spin-free information is hard to come by in the world of policy professionals, where each fact is a piece of ammunition in the political battle. Even though the division between research and communication is clearly present in the minds and practices of policy professionals, most of them straddle the borderland between these two activities in their framing of social problems.

If framing problems is one aspect of policy professionals' skills, a second important aspect consists of knowing the political game: knowing *where* in the complex political system decisions are really made, *when* you have to act in the policy process, and *how* political actors think and act. This is the political specialists' particular advantage over lay actors, and the one Robert Dahl warned about as a potential perversion of democracy (Dahl 1989: 364ff). In order to fully obtain this particular form of knowledge, people often need a stint in the heart of the government apparatus – the government offices. And the largest benefit of this knowledge is perhaps reaped once they have left the government offices to work for other interests, such as PR agencies, private firms, or interest organizations.

A Swedish PR consultant maintains that this insider knowledge is invaluable in the current work:

> I've worked with national politics. I've worked with European politics. I've worked in the European Parliament, at the Department of Finance, and I've worked with international politics. /.../ So I've learned processes at a very high level in that way. How a government works, how European collaboration works, at the ministerial level. /.../ It gives you a tremendous insight into the political game ... and all that is something I have use for here. How a politician functions, how they interact, how decisions are made in everything from a political party to a lobbying organization. I've been part of political receptions many times /.../ as an advisor to a politician. So I've seen lobbying from all angles. I've seen media life. I was there when things got rough for my politicians, I've seen them /.../ agonize before government reshuffles and all that. It has been very instructive, and all this is useful now. All this is something others need to know.

Insider knowledge about politics such as that described here is impossible to get from textbooks. It takes on-the-job experience of a broad and deep kind to acquire it, and it is restricted to a few hundred people in a country such as Sweden. A political director at a trade union, because of her previous experience in the government offices, similarly knows how to 'find the right way in the system', knows whom to contact and at what stage. The government offices and the state bureaucracy 'are not a big mush to me: I know who to call by name and number. And that is such a big help when you are in a situation when you are trying to influence the right person.'

Knowing the nooks and crannies of politics and policy making is therefore a fundamental aspect of the necessary skills of a policy professional. This is also the most important skill that the lobbying firms buy when they employ ex-politicians and ex-political advisors. Knowing *people* is important, but not as important as knowing the *processes* and being able to talk in the right way to the right people. A communication advisor in The Hague explains:

> Some lobbyists are very proud of their personal political contacts in The Hague, usually they also have a political colour and now when the Liberals are in charge the lobbyists with the liberal colour think that they are one step ahead. But I don't think that's really interesting. Politicians come and go. I used to have excellent contact with all politicians in energy. We could call each other day and night, get drunk, whatever. But they are all gone now. /.../ So there come new people that don't

necessarily trust you, so the best skill you can have in The Hague is to be able to talk the language of politicians. I have to seduce them to take notice of my clients' views and positions. But we also have to look at 'what's in it for the politicians?'

Being able to talk in the right way and to know whom to talk to is one of the most valuable assets for a policy professional. In Europe, lobbying and other attempts to affect political outcomes rarely involve implicit or explicit threats. Much more often they entail finding common ground and making clear to decision makers that they actually have something important to gain from taking the lobbying party's perspective on board.

There are plenty of examples of such 'friendly' lobbying. A Dutch communication advisor (she prefers that title to 'lobbyist') explains how trying to influence things in the Netherlands requires a very different style of lobbying from what she thinks is typical for the US:

> I think also why lobbyists or political consultants are seen as an essential part in democracy is because they form a link between all of these different parties that come together to find a compromise, and in that regard I think political consultants here really are looking for that compromise instead of just 'winning'. /.../ We work for several American companies and it's ... a big part of our job is to explain that it doesn't work like this. 'No, you cannot do that.'
> *So they typically want to use their more confrontational style here as well?*
> Yes, yes.
> *And you just tell them that it's not going to work?*
> Yes.

From the other end of the exchange, helpful lobbyists are also appreciated and can get what they want by being helpful. A political advisor in the Dutch government says that although many lobbyists are crude and only articulate the narrow self-interest of their clients, which will get them nowhere, others are more resourceful and therefore more successful:

> You have really good lobbyists working here in The Hague and what they do is that they look at the viewpoints of the party and my interests and then they say 'Ok, where can we align our interests?' /.../
> *Are lobbyists successful in the Netherlands?*
> Yes, I think they are successful. And they are usually perceived as really negative and as kind of obscuring their influence and buying influence, buying laws, but I found that they can also be really of value because we don't have that much time or capacity here and they often know what the impact of a law would be. Then you can really use them to improve the policies and the laws that you're making here.

'I am a lobbyist, and I am here to help you' is the angle that will often get lobbyists through the door and sometimes even succeed in their endeavours. 'Do as I say, or else ...' will get them nowhere. This is something that US lobbyists transferring to Europe often will have to learn the hard way, by being shut out and ignored by policy makers. Successful lobbying in Europe has to seek and find common ground in order to be successful.

Knowing the processes and the appropriate language is important everywhere but becomes particularly imperative in the closed, opaque, and complex machinery of EU decision making (Laurens 2018: Ch. 4). A Swedish lobbyist describes the experience:

> Brussels is a hub – a sort of international melting pot – but in general I think you need lobbyists who know the culture and the semiotics of a topography. /.../ I think Brussels is initially completely impregnable. It took me some years before I grasped it. I can feel today that I have a great deal of experience with how an EU directive comes about. I can quite easily understand how a law comes about in Sweden, but the process of directives is completely different and a fair bit more complicated.

As described by lobbyists and political advisors in Brussels, it is very hard to gauge from the outside who exactly is involved in what stages of different decision-making processes in the Commission and other EU bodies. To make processes even more inaccessible to outsiders, EU institutions also use a particular lingo where, for example, seemingly vacuous terms take on very specific meanings in that particular context. Unless you are used to this, the risk that you will miss out on opportunities to affect outcomes is very large indeed. Again, what emerges most clearly is that you need to know processes and know how to speak the right language to be effective, while murky networks of political contacts are far less important.

But there is yet another aspect of knowledge production among policy professionals where access to people matters more: fast access to information and correct data. Often policy professionals need to know immediately where an issue lies at that moment, or they need to quickly get hold of some specific facts that can be used as political ammunition, and in collecting such information, personal networks are extremely important.

So the most important aspect of the personal networks is not that they give access and backchannels for influence but that they provide quick, almost frictionless, channels of information. A political advisor in Leinster House – the Irish parliament building – exemplifies the importance of personal networks for accessing information, where you could ask, 'Who do we know inside on single farm payments, or who do we know inside organics that we can ring? Who is somewhat sympathetic to Fianna Fail or somewhat sympathetic to Fine Gael? There would always be someone.'

His Latvian colleague concurs that the prime motive for having a large personal network is to secure access to information:

> That's why I have a lot of friends, and in Latvia it's very important to have contacts. Sometimes if you don't know, I know whom to call to get some information: Who can help me? And if he cannot help me he can suggest another person that can help me. /.../ The office has 11 workers but it's too small. They cannot know everything. Therefore it's important that you have a network and can go outside and ask the others, and maybe the others that are not directly working here can give you advice from the outside.

Friends are useful not because you can call them to try to change their minds, or because you can use them to open a back entrance to rooms where decisions are made. No, they are useful mostly because they know stuff that is useful to you. They are the fastest route to finding out what is taking place or what the facts are about a case. And that is regardless of whether you work inside or outside government. If you are on the inside you want to know what is going on among the organizations that are or will be affected by your decisions; if you are on the outside you need to know how decisions emerge from the inside. And then you need to know whom to call, be sure they actually answer, and feel confident you can trust their information.

Handling information can be dangerous. Accessing and providing fast and correct information is a game with little tolerance for even the smallest mistake. Any trivial mistake will immediately be used by your opponents to try to undermine your credibility. Being only half right is sometimes worse than telling a blatant lie. Many policy professionals enjoy the quick pace of their work, but the flipside is a constant fear of making mistakes that will expose 'their' politician, organizational representative, or client to attacks.

Policy professionals are often dependent on the public administration to provide fast and accurate information. But the information game has a reverse aspect: public officials sometimes become dependent on policy professionals, in particular lobbyists, for information about the actual state of affairs. Civil servants and other public administrators cannot know everything that is relevant for policy making in their particular section. This goes especially for technically complicated subject areas, where the strongest experts are often found in the industry of the sector. This is particularly pronounced in a complex environment such as the European Commission (EC) and other EU bodies (Laurens 2018). It is also the case that, for an administrative body with such a large mandate and geographical coverage as the EC, the organization is quite small and chronically understaffed (Tömmel 2014: Ch. 11). Hence, the civil servants at the Commission become quite dependent on outside expertise, and this is where the lobbyists enter:

> The difference between home and here is that it is so much easier to work as a lobbyist compared to back home in Sweden. In Sweden you always have the state apparatus; the state apparatus has a very deep knowledge, with expertise at a very detailed level, to which decision makers can turn to get their information. The difference here is that you have extremely competent people that work for the Commission, but of course they are not so many percentagewise. I mean, here they have 500 million people to take care of, at home we have 10 million, and I think the number of public administrators in Sweden is perhaps around 120 000? Down here there are 40 000 that take care of 500 million. This then implies that if you can deliver a trustworthy and fact-based message, or basis, then it is much easier to communicate down here than is the case in Sweden. I wasn't aware that it was so much easier, that the ways to make things work were so different down here compared to back home in Sweden.

The personnel scarcity at the EC leads to information scarcity, which necessitates relying on outside expertise, which opens the door ajar for lobbyists. Another way to look at it is that the public organizational density highly affects policy professionals' opportunities. In strong states such as Sweden, or for that matter the Netherlands or Ireland, opportunities to affect the course of events simply by presenting facts that are relevant for policy makers are fewer and harder to come by. In situations with scarcer public organization resources, opportunities arise. And if it is the case, as it is in Brussels, that lobbying organizations are many and well resourced, then the information game is stacked in favour of private interests (Laurens 2018).

Framing problems, knowing the game, and accessing and providing information are necessary ingredients for successful action among policy professionals. But the composition of these skills varies among individuals and positions. A distinction may be drawn between what in political journalistic parlance is known as 'hacks' and 'wonks' (Reed 2004). Hacks are political actors who are mostly interested in the political game for its own sake, who are focused on selling political standpoints to the public and the media, and who see communication as the core of politics. Wonks are people who are mostly interested in building institutions and policies, who focus on formulating long-term ideas and reform plans, and who think analysis is the core of politics and policy making (Medvetz 2012: 173–4, Reed 2004).

A typical wonk relies mostly on the ability to frame problems, using science and research in order to promote their ideas. For a wonk, the political game, including communication and selling, is something that has to be endured, a necessary evil to get the ideas across. For the hacks, the political game is what makes their hearts beat faster, while content sometimes takes a secondary role. You have to sell whatever is necessary in order to win debates and elections. Process expertise is essential and information access is important, while the ability to formulate problems is less central for the hack. The difference may be illustrated by these two Dutch political advisors, working for the same political party but with wonkish and hackish orientations respectively:

> Sometimes it's all game and it's ... there is not a win-win. You're just trying to ... it's not about the content anymore, it's only about the game and about hurting other parties in order to make yourself look good. Those are the weeks that I hate. (Advisor 1)

> *Do you feel that you have any influence today on the standpoints that the party is taking?*
> I hope not too much on the standpoints but on the way we translate the research /.../ and the way you frame it to the voters.
> *Does that mean in terms of packaging what arguments you use?*
> What arguments, which issues to attack at what time, which party leaders to attack on what weaknesses. (Advisor 2)

These differences in orientation are real and sometimes alluded to by policy professionals themselves. As a Swedish political advisor stated, '[In] the American debate, there are those "hacks" and "wonks", and I am a wonk.' At the same time, it is important not to overstate the distinction. Most policy professionals need to be a little of both in their daily work or over the course of their careers.

It is important to note that lobbyists (such as private political consultants, public affairs officers, communication advisors, etc.) are not fundamentally different from everybody else in these respects. Other policy professionals often like to think of themselves as fundamentally different from lobbyists. The latter work in a stigmatized line of business, but a closer look at what lobbyists do reveals that they basically apply exactly the same skill set and action repertoire as other policy professionals (see also Chapter 6). As we will find in Chapter 4, this also goes for their motivations, which are largely similar to those of other policy professionals. The difference lies more in the commitment to particular clients, which tends to be on a more fleeting and short-term basis for the lobbyists. But just like their policy professional counterparts in other types of organizations, they need to be able to frame problems, they know the political game from the inside and from experience, and they know how to find fast and reliable information.

NETWORKS: RECIPROCITY AND DIVERSITY

Since networks are so important to many policy professionals there is reason to delve somewhat further into their use of networks and what that use implies. This is where the boundary-spanning characteristics of policy professionals are especially pertinent, since their actions transcend their specific organizational attachments and articulate actors across a whole organizational landscape. Building and maintaining such networks therefore requires social skills of a particular kind.

At the core of networks lies the importance of trust. Information will only be shared with those who cannot be suspected of misusing it, and the information provided must be trusted by the receiver to be of any value. Since little in the way of formal credentials exists for the policy professional field, personal reputation is of paramount importance. In this way, as in many others, the policy professional field actually resembles the pre-modern world where a man's (sic!) honour and reputation were the most important social assets (Lappalainen 2017).

But policy professionals do not need to be mafiosan 'men of honour' ready to use violence, they need only to have a reputation for being serious, reliable, honest, and friendly. Such a reputation is particularly important for lobbyists, who have to convince clients to trust them and policy makers to listen to them. Hence, the successful lobbyist has to be the ultimate schmoozer without coming across as intrusive or a drag:

> Having personal relationships is important because people will trust you more if it works out and you know the person quite well and you have a good [relationship]. /.../ Somebody that you know on a personal level and that you maybe had a pint with a month ago, if you're ringing them up to say 'Could you help me?', 'Would you mind saying who is the person I should meet about this?', 'Could you help me yourself?', 'Do you think there is any chance of progressing ...?' or 'Is that any priority of the government or is it way down the list?' Just small indicators that you can pick up on the back of what I would call 'good personal relationships'. Then again, that has to be done delicately; you cannot overdo that. (Lobbyist, Ireland)

In this quote, we find not only the focus on acquiring information as the most important aspect of a network. It also focuses on the personal aspects of the networks and on the importance of building trust. And it also pinpoints the importance of not overusing the network so as not to wear network contacts out or make them feel exploited.

To be a successful networker and to build trust therefore also includes reciprocity. No one wants to be exploited, and the networker who only takes and takes without giving will soon find that the network has expired. You need to offer the other party something, or they will start to feel exploited in the long run:

> I think I build very strong networks so people never decline when I ask something. Because I always try to give them something in return and to make it good for them. Because when I invite them they will have influence; I make sure that they have influence so it won't be a waste and I make sure that when they attend a meeting

they'll hear something that is of value to them so I won't waste their time. (Director at a think tank, the Netherlands)

Reciprocity is a basic human orientation, probably hardwired into our brains over the millennia when cooperation was the only means to survival (Bowles and Gintis 2013, Fehr and Gintis 2007). Non-reciprocal relations (between adults) are most often seen as exploitation and create (often physical) discomfort and anger. No wonder policy professionals are so eager to maintain reciprocity in their network relations, or at least the impression of it.

To be efficient in helping the policy professional, networks need to be diverse. Echo chambers are of little value in acquiring relevant information. You need people located in various places who can provide information from a broad spectrum of issues and standpoints. A Swedish political advisor explicates:

> If we had the money, maybe we would have employed these people. Now we don't have money. But then you have to secure the flow of information. I want to find out things quickly as hell. And it's damn good if you want to find out things. I know someone who works for [the blue-collar trade union] LO, I know someone who works in parliament. I know someone who works for the EU Commission. I know someone who works just about anywhere. Then I can call and check: 'What about this?' It is a question of favours and returning favours.

Similarly, a Dutch think-tanker thinks that the breadth and diversity of his personal network was a key factor when he was offered his current position:

> I had a broad network of all kinds of people working from Christian [perspectives], a more or less orthodox worldview, in organizations, in all kinds of organizations: education, housing, care, and also in political parties. So I knew my counterparts, I knew them personally, in the other scientific institutes.

As shown by these two quotes, there has to be some sort of founding affinity with other network members, in the first case based on left-wing politics and in the other on a Christian affiliation. But beyond such affinity – without which there could be no personal network in the first place – networks need to be really diverse. They need to include people with different backgrounds but above all people who work in different organizations and therefore know different things. Piecing information together is a hard game if all the pieces look the same. Sociologist Mark Granovetter famously characterized this as 'the strength of weak ties', pointing to the importance of non-redundant sources in acquiring useful information (Granovetter 1973). But in the policy professional world such weak ties still need to be based on ideological affinity, since little information will be shared with adversaries.

Given the importance of personal networks, one might suspect that all policy professionals systematically engage in network building. But here a more varied picture emerges from the interviews. Some policy professionals certainly engage heavily in network building and even find considerable enjoyment in it. A political advisor in the Netherlands explains how it works:

> I started with that during my studies, so I did these extra-curricular activities where they told us that it would be very good if you built your network. So every person I met during those activities and who was someone I thought of as someone who would be important in my further career, I tried to approach on LinkedIn, for example. So I built the network just to be in touch ... to have the possibility to be in touch with each other, and I tried to do that through my internships as well as my work here. You meet so many people from all kinds of organizations, lobbyists ... you name it and we have met them, probably! So yes, it's a conscious decision.

Others, however, invest little in network building and let networks emerge spontaneously from their everyday work. Such policy professionals rely mainly on their academic expert skills and less on their connectedness in their daily work. For these people, having a network is useful (and nice), but it is not essential to their efficiency in daily work. They know how to frame problems, they know the political system regardless of who happens to be in office, and they know where to look for information that is not dependent on knowing the right people.

Networks are less formally regulated and hierarchical than organizations (Ahrne 2018), but that does not mean that they are devoid of status. To be the one who is approached rather than the one who approaches conveys more status and therefore more personal satisfaction. A political advisor in the Netherlands notes with satisfaction that 'people tend to come to me more than I tend to go to them' when he discusses how relations between political advisors from different parties work in the government offices. A long-standing presence in the corridors of power, he knows that people need him more than he needs them, and it gives him a certain pride, although of a modest and subdued kind.

Apart from conveying status, networks forge solidarity. Networks are often based on ideological affinities and shared issues, and through network interaction, bonds are established that can sometimes even trump organizational loyalty. Policy professionals who are concerned about, say, gender, the environment, or entrepreneurship sometimes find that their networks are much more congenial to their endeavours than the organizations that employ them. At the same time, it is the organization, and not the network, that employs them, which makes a certain restraint necessary. Organizational leaders want those they employ to be working for them, as the organization's representative in networks, and not the other way around.

Network building is facilitated by physical proximity, and in this regard policy professionals are blessed. The political world is small and geographically restricted to 'this square mile', as a political advisor in a government building in The Hague calls his professional world. His Irish colleague concurs: 'You just keep meeting the same figures over and over again so the pool is quite small in terms of the number of people involved and whatnot. And the links are quite close.'

Not only are the political circles of the capital city small, the smallness of the countries in question is also emphasized as facilitating network building, sometimes in amusing ways. For example, when an Irish political consultant exclaims that 'Ireland is a small face and you know that six degrees of separation is more like three degrees of separation in Ireland,' she is echoed by her Latvian colleague, who claims that 'Latvia is pretty small and, you know the "six handshakes" theory, in Latvia I think it's two or three handshakes.' The Katzensteinian emphasis on the importance of smallness (see Chapter 1) is certainly shared by the actors in the policy professional field.

BECOMING A POLICY PROFESSIONAL

Where have policy professionals acquired their skills? As we noted in Chapter 2, there are no designated study programmes through which one becomes a policy professional, nor are there any formal requirements for becoming one. But somehow, necessary skills are still acquired somewhere. But where, and how?

There is hardly anyone who works as a policy professional who has no academic training. But interestingly, there are different opinions about how important any particular academic subject is for becoming a successful policy professional. Some of the interviewees argue that their specific knowledge in, say, econometric modelling or policy analysis, has been very useful in their position. But most argue that the specific subject content actually matters little, and that what matters are generic analytical and language skills. Policy professionals need to be able to digest texts and arguments quickly, cut to the bone of an extended argument, summarize a long document into five bullet points, and see the implications for their organization of a new report or an academic research programme. Such abilities are learned at universities and cannot easily be acquired elsewhere.

A manager at a trade union office in Sweden confirms that generic academic skills are what they are looking for in their employees, and that this implies looking for university graduates:

> I think you need these tools that you get in an academic education in order to achieve. Because I may come to you and say, 'We have found this report. Tomorrow

our chairperson will speak on this subject. Before you go home today, I want a two-page PM about what is important in this and what our organization should say based on what the report says.' You have to be very good at that. And then you can't start to fumble about for 'How do I do it? How do I distil the interesting parts?' but you have to use routinized methods – 'What are the conclusions? What is the background? How can I link this to our stuff and quickly get it down on paper?' /.../ You may be a terrific person but you won't be able to do it unless you are used to processing text. You have to be able to write long wordy texts that turn everything inside out, and you have to be able to distil that text to 'What are the most important five points in this?' That is quality. Those are high demands.

Even when supplied with generic academic skills, policy professionals need a large amount of on-the-job training in order to become efficient. They need to find out who is who, learn how issues have evolved in this particular organization over time, and understand the formal and informal power structures they need to relate to and many other things that simply cannot be seen from the outside.

Given this, one might have expected there to be structured induction programmes for different policy professional positions, and especially for those who work most closely to political power in the government offices. This is not typically the case, however. In fact, there is strikingly little induction into what is expected of a political advisor in government or parliament. New arrivals tend to dive in head first, or perhaps rather to be pushed into the deep end of the pool and told to swim. This can be a truly frightening experience, and they have to develop methods to cope:

> The only thing you can do is to talk to the one who was here before, but he's gone so he's not going to give you that much information. So if you start the first moment of the term and walk into office together with [the minister], then there is a formal introduction programme for the minister. /.../ But no, there is no introduction [for you]. So what I did is that in my first two weeks I made a lot of appointments with all the directors and the most important civil servants. They give advice, what they would like from you, but that is more self-education. (Dutch policy advisor in a ministry)

The scarcity of formal induction means that role models become very important. Policy professionals in the government offices and political parties look to their leading politicians – the ones who recruited and sometimes mentored them – to find clues on how to behave. Think-tankers, organizational experts, and consultants look to esteemed senior colleagues to find out what to do and how to do it.

Very few policy professionals have any use for their family experiences in providing preparation and guidance. Few come from 'political homes' in the sense that anyone in the family of origin held political office of any kind.

Even if many of their families discussed politics, few policy professionals had any derived experience of the inner workings of political life before they started their own careers. Instead, the most important aspect of the family of upbringing seems to be the instalment of certain values regarding hard work, reliability, and integrity. Although there may certainly be some degree of nostalgic embellishment in this, most can point to specific instances of how such values have been important to their own jobs and careers.

CONCLUSION: GENERIC SKILLS AND LOCAL APPLICATION

The application of the policy professional skills is very local, dependent on the context and knowledge about the relevant actors there. How have problems been framed before? How does the specific procedure work? Who knows what about what? For policy professionals, generic skills only become valuable in local application using local knowledge and information. In this sense, the knowledge base of policy professionals is much more circumscribed than, for example, academic knowledge. The latter can easily be applied successfully in other national contexts. The sociology professors in Stockholm could move next week to Washington, DC, and apply virtually everything they know in the new context. The same would go for a surgeon or an engineer. This is not at all the case for policy professionals; very little of what they know can be successfully applied outside the specific context in which they are embedded. A policy professional that moved from The Hague to Stockholm would have to start almost from scratch, building networks and trying to understand who is who and what is what in an unfamiliar place.

If the application of various skills is so dependent on local networks and local information, why are the skills themselves so generic? Why is what policy professionals do so similar across contexts?

One possible answer could be that similarities are the results of diffusion processes, so that successful and/or legitimate practices in one context are transferred to and applied in other contexts. Organizational research has put much emphasis on such diffusion processes across organizational and institutional contexts (Drori, Meyer, and Hwang 2006).

However, this does not seem to be the most important explanation. Policy professionals rarely refer to experiences elsewhere when they explain what they do and why they do it. In no interviews have I encountered policy professionals pointing to influences from elsewhere to explain what they do and why. Instead, as pointed out, many of them are quite curious as to what takes place in Sweden and in other places where I interviewed.

Even lobbying, which could be expected to be greatly affected by global trends and techniques, is highly contextual. As discussed, this is shown more precisely in the form of a particular European style of lobbying and influence work. Lobbying in European style means offering something useful for the counterpart, which can be contrasted to the more confrontational US style of lobbying (Woll 2012). It means searching for common ground, finding out what the political decision maker wants and needs, and trying to find out where interests might be aligned.

Instead of diffusion, the main explanation for similarity is found in the architecture of political power, which is very much the same across contexts. Beyond differences related to historical traditions and political-institutional frameworks, political power is structured in similar ways in various capital cities. Therefore, what policy professionals do becomes very similar. They need to frame problems in certain ways, they need to know the political game (which in itself looks very much the same in all democratic contexts), and they need to find fast and yet reliable information from civil servants and from other policy professionals. And this they need to do regardless of which party system is in place or how political resources are distributed among actors.

This does not mean that there are no differences at all across national contexts. As we will find in later chapters, motivations for becoming a policy professional rather than an elected politician vary according to the electoral system one is embedded in, and the careers of policy professionals are also affected by the institutional and organizational structures. But the daily handiwork among policy professionals looks strikingly similar in places as different as Brussels and Riga. To the curious policy professional who wants to know how it works in other places I can only say: You may understand political power, but you are not as special as you'd like to think.

REFERENCES

Ahrne, Göran. 2018. 'The Organization of Action.' In *Concepts in Action*, edited by Håkon Leiulfsrud and Peter Sohlberg, pp. 172–88. Leiden: Brill.

Bowles, Samuel, and Herbert Gintis. 2013. *A Cooperative Species: Human Reciprocity and its Evolution*. Princeton, NJ: Princeton University Press.

Dahl, Robert A. 1989. *Democracy and Its Critics*. New Haven, CT: Yale University Press

Drori, Gili S., John W. Meyer, and Hokyu Hwang, eds. 2006. *Globalization and Organization: World Society and Organizational Change*. Oxford: Oxford University Press.

Fehr, Ernst, and Herbert Gintis. 2007. 'Human Motivation and Social Cooperation: Experimental and Analytical Foundations.' *Annual Review of Sociology* 33: 43–64.

Granovetter, Mark S. 1973. 'The Strength of Weak Ties.' *American Journal of Sociology* 78 (6): 1360–80.

Lappalainen, Tomas. 2017. *Världens första medborgare: om statens uppkomst i det antika Grekland*. Stockholm: Lind & Co.

Laurens, Sylvain. 2018. *Lobbyists and Bureaucrats in Brussels. Capitalism's Brokers.* New York: Routledge.

Medvetz, Thomas. 2012. *Think Tanks in America.* Chicago, IL: University of Chicago Press.

Michels, Robert. 1911. *Political Parties: A Sociological Study of the Oligarchical Tendencies of Modern Democracy* . Reprinted in 1962. New York: Free Press.

Reed, Bruce. 2004. 'Bush's War Against Wonks: Why The President's Policies are Falling Apart.' *Washington Monthly*, http://www.washingtonmonthly.com/features/2004/0403.reed.html (accessed 15 November 2018).

Tömmel, Ingeborg. 2014. *The European Union: What It Is and How It Works.* London: Palgrave.

Woll, Cornelia. 2012. 'The Brash and the Soft-Spoken: Lobbying Styles in a Transatlantic Comparison.' *Interest Groups & Advocacy* 1 (2): 193–214.

4.   Power without responsibility

She comes across as a bit dishevelled, where we sit in a local bar that gets noisier and noisier as the after-work crowd starts pouring in. She is currently 'between jobs', as the euphemism goes, and recounts her recent experiences from the government offices:

> It's like being dropped into a very dysfunctional family. /.../ The difficult part of it is to explain to other people the intensity that formed my every day. It's one thing to say that there were long days, there were endless weeks as there was no such thing as a weekend, but it was full-on, you know, everything mattered! It was not like you would just go on in there on ... everything just had the potential to bring that disaster. You just couldn't keep your eyes off ... even the mundane things. You'd realize that they were mundane and go 'why am I going to ... but this has the potential to just escalate.' So that level of concentration. /.../
> *It must be like you are soldiers coming back from war zones and then adjusting to normal life?*
> Absolutely! You'd go for drink sessions or meetings with your colleagues 'because they've been to 'Nam, they know'. You can tell the people, but they don't understand. You want to spare them the details.

And still she thinks they were the happiest days of her life: 'Whatever I said about it: It was a huge privilege, and for me not coming from a political background it was an absolute fluke that I got access to that level.'

She could have been from anyplace: Ireland, Latvia, Sweden, or the Netherlands. I suspect her story would have been pretty much the same had she come from Germany or Britain or the US. It is a story about the lure of power, the attraction of being in the midst of events, even as you become worn down and stressed out. A story about having influence without attention or ultimate responsibility.

In this chapter I will delve into the motivations of policy professionals and the particular attractions in their line of work. Their relation to political power, and the different aspects of such power, is the starting point of the analysis. I will then ask why these political actors prefer to be policy professionals rather than elected politicians and how they view people who hold elected office. The last theme to be covered in the chapter deals with commitment and loyalty among policy professionals. In contrast to the last chapter, in which similarities across national contexts were emphasized, this chapter highlights how institutional differences, in particular those related to the political system in the broad sense, affect policy professionals' ambitions and motivations.

THE LURE OF POWER

If a single word were to be used to summarize the motivations of policy professionals and the perceived attractions in their line of work, it would have to be *power*. Policy professionals are – just as much as the principals they serve – political creatures, for which the pursuit of political power is a key driver. Many of them perceive that they actually have power, and enjoy this fact. A political advisor for a political party in the Netherlands is asked if he has had any influence over the issues of the political party he serves. He is unassuming and low-key in his appearance, and yet this is how he sees his role and position:

> I have had a great deal of influence, yes. I managed to influence all the major events that have happened in the past 30 years that our party was involved in.
> *And if you compare your influence to a member of parliament?*
> I think it's equal.
> *Is it equal in the sense that it's the same kind of influence, or is it a different kind of influence?*
> It's different because I'm not the person that people know. So my influence is on the inside. But in doing so it's still important because when I work in a proper way with our political leader, I have been able to make them do in a way … what they did.

There are several noteworthy aspects of this quote that this chapter will delve further into. One is that the advisor claims that he actually has as much power as high-level elected representatives of the party. Formally an underling to the elected representatives, in reality he is just as empowered as they are. The second thing to note is that the very invisibility of his power is an important aspect of it. The fact that few people on the outside even know of his existence is of little concern to this particular professional, and as we will find in this chapter, many policy professionals actually see invisibility as a great advantage of their line of business. If people do not know you exist, they will not bother you, and being bothered is not something policy professionals strive for. The last noteworthy thing about this quote is that the advisor clearly works *for* the party leadership but *towards* (and possibly sometimes *against*) regular MPs. 'I made them do what they did' is what he actually claims, in a matter-of-fact, low-key kind of way.

The whole field in which policy professionals dwell is suffused with political power. Hence, it is no surprise that power figures so prominently in their motivations and in the attractions of this occupational niche. But a closer look at exactly what power – and power over what – motivates policy professionals reveals a less obvious picture. What emerges from the interviews is that there

are at least three different ways in which power is central to the policy professionals. Policy professionals are typically motivated by all three aspects of
power, although their relative weight varies substantially among individuals.
One is power as *agency*, the ability to affect decisions and outcomes. Here, the
attraction lies in being able to forge history, even if sometimes in small ways.
Making a difference is what counts, regardless of whether this comes in the
form of designing a major public policy change or only in getting a certain
perspective into tomorrow's newspaper.

'Being in government is so much more rewarding in terms of what you can
achieve and what you can deliver,' explains an Irish political advisor, and
a colleague from another party concurs: 'I enjoy politics as a skill and politics
as a practical input of things. You do get a thrill out of writing a good speech
and listening to it being read out. I enjoy seeing a policy paper that I have
worked on being published, then maybe some legislation from that being
pushed at.' And regardless of country or position, the joy of being able to make
a difference suffuses the policy professionals' view of their work. That is why
so few of them would consider an academic career. Academia is seen as distant
from the real action, from being able to affect the course of events, from seeing
one's ideas put into practice: 'You could say whatever you wanted, but nobody
was listening' is how a Dutch think-tanker laconically summarizes his experiences from the world of research. It is also why so few policy professionals
want to become civil servants: 'I had worked for 10 years in so-called "neutral
advice" and I was bored with that, because you always do that from a certain
normative standpoint and I longed to be explicit about that,' as another Dutch
think-tanker puts it. A policy professional is seldom satisfied with providing
neutral advice on policy alternatives; they burn for political change, and power
as agency is key to all they do.

The second aspect of the attractions of power is the *proximity*, being close to
power and to the spaces and circles where important decisions are made. The
government offices offer the closest proximity to power, with all the ensuing
buzz and excitement. This is often noticed most clearly by those who have
been forced to leave because their party has lost the election or their minister
has resigned. Many people long to go back to the glory days in the government
offices. But even for those still in the government offices, proximity to power
offers a buzz, as put by this advisor to the Latvian government: 'It's like …
how to say? Like a trip. /…/ And this you cannot buy at the market.'

His feelings are seconded by a former political advisor in Sweden, looking
back on his former job from his current position as political consultant:

> Maybe what I miss now is being in the midst of events. With all of these things
> happening. /…/ It is really a matter of life and death, almost. 'This has to be solved.'

'Here is a proposal, we have to take a stand.' It is fast, it is serious – 'This will decide Swedish politics here and now.'

The proximity to power is greatest in the government offices, where meeting ministers from one's own and other governments is a run-of-the-mill experience. But in such a powerhouse it is sometimes hard to make one's own voice heard and one's own contribution matter. Power as agency and power as proximity therefore stand in a complicated relationship to one another. One can only experience the attraction of proximity to power if that power is real, that is, if it embodies power as agency. But in places with large concentrations of power as agency, it may be hard to be a power agent oneself. So sometimes there is a trade-off between power as proximity and power as agency: it is not necessarily at the very hub of power that it is easiest to affect the course of events.

Even if the lure of power as proximity is strongest in the government offices, it is far from absent in other policy professional positions. For example, lobbyists and other political consultants enjoy the glamour that is sometimes found in their line of work. They sometimes follow their clients into the highest circles of power, they often work in fancy downtown offices, and they enjoy being in the midst of events. They can often work directly with higher management in private companies and they lobby the inner circles of government. It is exciting and has a certain 'wow' factor when brought up as dinner conversation.

The third aspect is perhaps more mundane. It concerns power as *self-determination*, being able to define one's own expressed standpoints, strategies, and daily work. This is conspicuous in the way many policy professionals argue about the importance of keeping control of what they say and do. This can sometimes be a challenge, since their employing organizations have their say in what message they think their policy professionals should convey. But policy professionals are typically reluctant to bias their message or say things that are blatantly untrue, since it devalues their credibility and worsens their future labour market value (see the discussion in Chapter 3), and they want to keep control of their own message. They would much rather be the puppeteer than the puppet.

The trade-off between power as self-determination and power as proximity or agency is palpable. In a small organization removed from the centre of power, it is easier to keep control over what you do, how you do it, and what you communicate about your arguments and findings. At the other end of the spectrum, a state secretary is very much circumscribed in what can be said and done, since everything will immediately reflect on the government. At the organizational pinnacles in the policy professional world, the personal contribution has to be tightly controlled in order to pursue power as agency and enjoy the proximity to power.

Power as agency, power as proximity, and power as self-determination are all key or even *necessary* ingredients in what makes the work of the policy professional attractive for those who pursue it. But power is hardly ever a *sufficient* driver for policy professionals. They are no Lyndon B. Johnsons, for whom power in and of itself is what keeps them going (Caro 1982–2012). They need intellectual stimulus in their pursuits, they need to feel that there is intellectual challenge and interest. But neither are they academics, for whom the search for truth is enough:

> It's Machiavelli and Kant, you know that both these are there. It's *geist und macht*. If you want just *geist*, then you should stay at university – and that I didn't want. I wanted to influence power, to speak the truth to power, but I also knew that you would have to fight for it and that you would not always win.

As put by this Dutch think-tanker, what matters is both being right, in the sense of having the stronger argument, and getting right, in the sense of actually winning. Winning without being right is empty, being right without winning is meaningless. Again, what comes across clearly is that being a policy professional is quite different from being an academic or an expert. But, as the next section will emphasize, it is also different from being an elected politician or organizational representative.

UNBEARABLE ELECTED POLITICS: COMMON THEME WITH NATIONAL VARIATIONS

So far, the comparative story of policy professionals has mainly emphasized similarities across national contexts. The skills of policy professionals and their application are quite similar in different settings, and the prime motivations regarding power also come across as strikingly similar across different institutional environments. But once we move to relations between policy professionalism and elected politics, and the specific relations between policy professionals and politicians, national differences come to the foreground. The political systems shape these particular aspects of policy professionals' motivations and career considerations to a considerable extent. Few policy professionals consider elected office as a desirable future for themselves, but the most important reasons why they find elected politics unattractive differ substantially between countries.

In *Sweden*, there are two main reasons why so few policy professionals would consider a future as an elected politician. The most common one is that, as many of them claim, they could never stand the personal media attention. The media scrutiny would be absolutely unbearable, claims a political secretary in parliament: 'It seems horrible.' A second political secretary prefers not having to endure 'the unbelievable unease there would be to get a camera in your face, even if it is a friendly camera'. And a think-tank employee reflects on the fact that as a politician 'you are never allowed to be anything more than humdrum, because then you get exposed in the media and your future becomes impossible', because 'it is so circumscribed today what you are allowed or not allowed to say'. 'I do not think I could stand it' is the short summary of why this person would not consider becoming an elected politician.

For those who have left party politics, this mass media exposure is a big reason why they wanted to leave. A person with long experience with parliament and government offices but who now works for a private company reflects on the world of politics and the road not chosen:

> *What do you think made you not want to do this, to try to become a minister, party leader, and get leading positions within [the party]?*
> I think it had very much to do with the fact that I worked as a close advisor to these people. And saw what a grind it was. /.../ You know, I was his chief of communication, and then I would call him early, early in the morning because then the first news programmes were starting. Should he have any comments on that? Should he have a TV crew coming out to his house? /.../ Should he have some statement at six o'clock in the morning, from his kitchen sofa more or less? And radio and such kept calling all the time. Then that was followed by newspaper interviews all day long. And then late in the afternoon, the TV talk shows called because then he was supposed to take part in [the political talk show] *Kvällsöppet* or a TV debate in Gothenburg at 22.30. And then on some flight to Gothenburg at 19.30 and back home 01.30 and straight to bed, and then it started all over again with me calling at 05.30 because there was some comment on [the radio news] *Dagens eko*. /.../ And journalists who all the time would look for weaknesses or some mistake and 'What about this?' And who were constantly poking around and checking our receipts and would look over them all the time and ask, 'What about these numbers?' and 'What is the matter with everything here?' /.../ To go to work every day knowing that there are 20 or 30 journalists out there who want nothing more than to shoot you down from your position. That is not how I feel when I come in to work here.

At the same time, the relations with the mass media are highly complex. When Swedish policy professionals were asked about what made them most happy and satisfied at work, such feelings were almost always connected to getting their message into the mass media, to hearing their own words from the minister's mouth on TV, to changing the public debate as conducted in the mass media (Svallfors 2017). Policy professionals have a very complex attitude towards the mass media, which they fear and loathe at the same time as they are very dependent on them for their daily information and mundane work satisfaction.

A second, almost as common, reason why policy professionals in Sweden shun the role of elected politician is that many of them hold many aspects of the practices of representative democracy in quite low regard. Such politics are seen as slow and boring, as shallow and media-driven, as filled with personal rivalry and petty malice.

The unbearable slowness of elected politics does not primarily concern the processes, where it may take a long time before the political system is able to come up with concrete proposals to bring things forward. But in this regard there is considerable understanding among policy professionals that democratic processes take time and that this is unavoidable. Instead, the most common Swedish complaint about the slow world of representative democracy is that politics in this form is too slow and boring as a *career*. As an elected politician, one has to start from the bottom and slowly work up the ladder to things that really matter. Many do not have time and patience for this, as argued by this political secretary:

> *Would you consider becoming an elected politician?*
> I really don't think so. /.../ I don't know, I wouldn't say absolutely no, but it is nothing that tempts me. What tempts me is the advisor role, that is what I think is most fun. Like this, behind the scenes, give recommendations, and so on.
> *What is it that doesn't tempt you then, about being a politician?*
> Partly it is the road to becoming a politician of the calibre where I think it would be fun. You know, local constituencies and sit and talk about … Not to belittle it, but I don't know … It is simply not anything that I am very interested in, to sit and talk about whether that dog yard should remain or not.

Policy professionals often perceive that the parties' ways of recruiting and promoting lack respect for knowledge and merit and that the way forward therefore becomes tedious and boring. A former political advisor who is now political director at a trade union thinks that '[my party] has to a large extent been based on – how should I put it – that you should sit a number of shitty years in order to get promoted on the lists', while going strictly by merit 'has never been [their] idea about how the political career should be ordered'. This political director lacks 'the patience to go the long way. I can do politics in a much more fun and fast way. I play a bigger role, I can influence more in this way.'

At the same time as elected politics is criticized for being too slow and boring, it is also considered to be too shallow. Complaints along these lines not only consider politics to be too media-driven and short-sighted, but many also see a sort of cold-hearted foxiness at the core of elected politics. A political secretary in parliament explains why it may be hard to find a comfortable place in politics: '[T]here is a shallowness in politics that is found in all parties. Tactics. Scheming. Both politically but also for personal benefit. That you have to choose your moments.' A political secretary at the local level claims that it was a painful insight to understand 'how much scheming' there was in the political system, how much lying and slandering, and 'that the biggest enemies are found in your own party'.

Although complaints about short-sighted politics and political infighting are heard also in the interviews from *Latvia*, almost nothing is said about political careers in leading elected positions being slow and boring. In Latvia, parties come and go, although familiar faces often turn up in new parties and constellations, and party memberships are small and fleeting (Pridham 2017). The step from being a think-tanker or political advisor to becoming a leading elected politician is, in principle, short and doable. No need here for years of tedious drudgery in a list-based semi-seniority system as in Sweden. A political landscape in constant flux constantly offers new opportunities for entering political life in quite prominent positions, for those so inclined.

But still, few Latvian policy professionals claim to strive to become a government minister, an MP, or a mayor. Why? Here it is the case that Latvian policy professionals tend to take an even dimmer outlook on the characteristics of parliamentary politics than their Swedish counterparts. Many see politicians as generally untrustworthy, incompetent, and scheming, and see parliament as a place of personal animosity and stale procedures. A political advisor who has just left the government offices (on adversarial terms, which might explain some extra frankness in the expressions) states his opinion about MPs:

> I think they are rather lazy, unfortunately. And not the brightest, unfortunately. Not all of them, but I would rather say that there is a small percentage that is trying to be productive, trying to change things and work for the [public's] benefit. But the big majority … I don't know what they are doing. They sit through their four years.

Another current advisor in parliament concurs that not all MPs are that impressive:

> I still have a huge respect for a few of them but I don't understand why some … with all my honour, you really did a great job a few years ago but now you're too old and you're not understanding anything of what's going on, and you are asking stupid questions about the state budget or if we have a deficit.

This criticism, bordering on disrespect, of the average elected politicians in general is rarely applied to the principal politicians that political advisors serve. Many claim that *their* politician is honest but that the average politician is not; *their* politician is competent, but the average politician is not. The extent to which this is a rationalization of the qualities of the politician who gave them their job and can dismiss them again, and the extent to which views about 'the others' are negatively biased is, of course, hard to tell. But it is an interesting case of individual pieces not adding up to the broader picture.

The scepticism about elected politicians is heard also in Sweden, but in the Latvian case there is an added element of a more systemic critique, that politics is contaminated by backroom deals and personalized conflicts. Latvian politics has a recent history of being quite corrupt, and although things were substantially improved over the course of the first decade of the new millennium, perceptions and images linger (Pridham 2017). The Latvian policy professionals burn for politics and for changing society, but they typically do not see parliament as the right place to make that happen. They would rather try to affect policy making through their advisory role, in parties, government, or civil society.

When we turn the gaze to *Ireland*, a third variant of unbearable politics appears. In the Irish case this may be summarized under the headline 'the tyranny of localism'. The local constituencies become extremely important in a political system such as Ireland's, with multi-member constituents and where the motto 'all politics is local' is taken to an extreme (Collins and O'Shea 2003). An elderly think-tanker reflects on why he would never consider going into politics:

> If my children came to me and said that they're going into Irish politics, I would advise them against it. The lifestyle is terrible!
> *Why is that?*
> The constituency pressure. For Irish politicians, family life is awful. Why do they do it?
> *Do they get phone calls late at night with angry people from the local constituency?*
> Maybe not angry people, but they get people calling them at all hours, day and night. I do remember that my father was an official but we'd have people calling to the house, you know. He was never off duty. I think that, given the pressure on politicians, they're doing quite well actually, but it's a terrible life.

A political advisor concurs and puts it all down to the particular election system, with multi-member districts, which makes local constituents extremely important:

> You are incredibly close to your voters and your community. And you have to be because of the [election system] and everything that has to do with that. So it's kind of you get the product of the system you have. /.../ 'You're my TD [i.e., MP], you should sort it out, and if you don't sort it out I have three other TDs that might sort it out and then I'm going to give them my number one.' /.../ I would say that it's more skewed towards constituency, and the constituency piece is what I find the least interesting.

MPs from Ireland – and their assistants – are often occupied with securing benefits for their local constituents. It could be in the form of facilitating access to health care and social services, or trying to make sure that national facilities end up in their particular constituency. The late political scientist Peter Mair characterized the Irish system as amounting to 'amoral localism',[1] and many Irish policy professionals share his misgivings about the aggregated effects of excessive localism. They also tend to regard such work as menial and below their competence, they avoid doing constituency service when they can, and they would not dream of running for elected office since it involves pandering to local needs and demands rather than looking at the bigger picture.

However, a minority of policy professionals – who are actually posted in the local constituencies – actually see something valuable in the current localism, and they enjoy taking part in it. 'I'm needed here,' summarizes one parliamentary assistant's explanation for why he likes doing community work, and a second assistant claims that 'you can have someone coming into the constituency office and saying, "Oh, my medical card has been removed. Can you help me?" and I like that because you can get a good result.' A third summarizes the benefits of the current system:

> For me at least it reflects the Irish political system. So the idea is like yes, politicians in Ireland have to do a lot of constituency work. But is that not democracy? Is that not the idea that someone be represented by their representative? So it's quite unique and people don't like it sometimes but I kind of see the value in it. When you see people that need help and they get help.

For policy professionals such as this one, political localism is not a problem at all. On the contrary, it is the very essence of politics to help people in their everyday lives. For this political assistant, politics is not mainly about devising policies and implementing them on a national scale; it is about listening to people's small concerns and helping them get on with their lives. He finds morality where Peter Mair found amorality, clientelism is given an appealing touch, and he comes across as an ardent defender of the current system and practices. But as shown, many other policy professionals in Ireland beg to disagree, and argue that this localism is the main reason why they prefer to stay out of elected office. It is of course hard to tell whether these differences among Irish policy professionals are caused by different personalities being selected to different positions or if it is different experiences in different settings (local constituents vs. the political circles in Dublin) that forge different outlooks.

Compared to policy professionals in the other three countries, those in the *Netherlands* on the whole express less negativism about elected politics and elected office. Compared to Sweden, relatively little is heard about the unbearable media frenzy or about politics as a slow and boring career. Compared to those in Latvia, Dutch policy professionals see their politicians in a fairly positive light, or at least not as incompetent and dishonest. Compared to Ireland, there is no excessive localism making elected office hard to stomach. And compared to the other three countries, it is more common among Dutch MPs to have a background that includes some policy professional experience: about 40 per cent of Dutch MPs in 2017 report some previous policy professional position in their CVs, which is more than what is found in Latvia (27 per cent), Sweden (22 per cent), or Ireland (11 per cent).[2] Dutch policy professionalism is to a somewhat larger extent than elsewhere a training ground for becoming an MP, and Dutch policy professionalism seems somewhat less strongly separated from elected politics than in the other countries.

And yet, many Dutch policy professionals express little desire to ever become MPs or government ministers. Why is that? Here, again, the answer may be sought in the political system characteristics of the country. Dutch politics is filled with compromise and deals. The election system, with very low thresholds for parties to enter parliament, makes for permanent minority and coalition governments. This tendency to scramble for the middle and for broad consensus is also reinforced by Dutch political history, where elite compromise and consensus became necessary to bridge deep-seated religious and cultural divisions in Dutch society (Lijphart 1968). Even though the institutional underpinnings of this 'pillar system' are now long gone, a political-cultural orientation towards compromise remains. All in all, in the eyes of many policy professionals, this constant search for consensus and the middle ground makes electoral politics a bit bland and diffuse, devoid of strong ideological components and arguments.

At the same time, many Dutch political advisors and other policy professionals deplore the mediatized, personalized, and conflict-ridden character of parliamentary life and elected politics more broadly. Perhaps as a paradoxical effect of the compromise-oriented political culture when it comes to substantive issues, politicians running for office often turn to making elections a question of personal appeal and charisma. At least this is the picture that many policy professionals paint, and it makes the thought of running for elected office unattractive. A party think-tanker explains why going into parliament would not be an attractive prospect:

> You have to love to go to all of these debates, to all these people locally, to go to television [and] radio. If I state it a little bit cynically I would say that you have to love, a little bit, to hear yourself speak, to have a little a bit of ... *Narcissism?*
> Yes. And I think that the work that they are doing is very important and people, all the people that I have met, also from other parties, 90% of them are people who are dedicated and they are motivated because of the governmental good. Not because of their own agenda or their own career. But to do the work that you need to do you have to love a little bit ... almost acting, a little bit to be on stage, on show. And me, myself, I think I get too little satisfaction out of doing that. I think that other people can do that better than I do.

This is perhaps the quintessential policy professional we hear in this quote. Preferring the back stage to the front stage, feeling uneasy about exposure and visibility. These are common policy-professional orientations, but perhaps they are heard more often in the Netherlands because here policy professionals typically have fewer fundamental complaints about how elected politics work. If elected politics is fundamentally sound, your own decision to stay out of it comes down to personal taste and style.

To sum up, we can clearly see how the character of party structures and electoral systems affects the particular reasons why most policy professionals prefer their way of doing politics to the alternative route of running for and holding elected office. At the same time, it is important to keep in mind that the general perception that the policy professional mode of doing politics is faster and more fun is common to a majority of policy professionals, regardless of country. Some policy professionals, particularly among political advisors, see their job as a training ground for eventually taking the helm themselves. But most of them see policy professionalism as an attractive *alternative* for those who want to engage in politics without having to endure elected politics.

One question still remains concerning the national differences in policy professionals' outlook on elected politics. That is the question of why Swedish policy professionals seem to be so much more bothered by potentially inquis- itive mass media than their colleagues elsewhere. The feelings that elected office is unbearable because you become the centre of intrusive personal media scrutiny is pervasive in Sweden, but much less so in the other countries. I can find no immediate interpretation of this; it is unlikely that the Swedish mass media are much worse than elsewhere, or that personal political exposure would be greater in Sweden. Why this particular reason for shunning elected office is more prominent in Sweden than in the other countries remains puzzling.

Many policy professionals profess that they do not want to become elected politicians. But can we take them at their word? This could in principle just be a 'sour grapes' proposition. Perhaps they claim they do not want to become politicians because they have failed to gain political support and have to be satisfied with being advisors of one kind or another. This is of course hard to tell. But as we will find in the next chapter, at least they are true to their word in the sense that hardly anyone (at least in Sweden) gets into elected office within a five-year period. The policy professional career seems largely to be a parallel political career to the elected one, and in this section I have suggested that this is mainly because policy professionals do not *want* to become elected politicians, and that the reasons for this are, in turn, highly affected by the characteristics of the political system.

POLITICIANS: ADMIRED AND DESPISED

As shown in the previous section, many policy professionals point to deficiencies in elected politics as a reason for not wanting to become elected themselves. But do they actually consider themselves politicians (although of an unelected kind), or are they something else? This question is of course most pertinent for those who work closely with elected politicians, as political advisors in parties, parliaments, and governments.

Most policy professionals, including political advisors, claim that they are *not* politicians, that being a politician is something different from being an advisor. Politicians are people who voters have elected and who take actual decisions, and that is not what political advisors are, no matter how closely they work with politicians. At the same time, the line of division between politician and advisor is not that clear-cut in practice, as discussed in the previous chapter. Even some people who are sure they are not politicians – like this advisor in the Dutch parliament – become uncertain when the question is posed:

> *Do you see yourself as a kind of politician when you work here?*
> No … That's a hard question. No, I think a politician is … no, I don't think so.
> *Why is that? What makes you not a politician?*
> I guess in the end I'm something … someone who works for politicians, and that feels very different. Yes, there is quite a big difference between being a politician or working here. In that sense … I mean, a politician is responsible for anything that the party does basically, and in the end they have to sit in that parliament building and vote, and sometimes I would be very happy not to make decisions on certain subjects. That is a comfortable position.

That is a comfortable position. The comment is intended as ironic, but it actually cuts to the heart of why most policy professionals prefer their way of doing politics, and why most of them claim not to be politicians. Theirs is not the burden of taking the formal decisions and taking responsibility for them; theirs is the comfort of exercising political power without having to take full responsibility for one's words and deeds.

Other policy professionals, although they are a minority, claim that they actually are politicians, although of a special kind. A press secretary in the Swedish government offices maintains that they 'are just as much a politician as the minister is. In reality.' They take part in making decisions, and they actively influence people with power and position. A political secretary in parliament agrees and even says 'in what I am supposed to do at work, I don't really see the difference between my responsibility and that of the MP when it comes to taking part. And it is even stated in our job description – to take part in and have responsibility for political development and such things, for example.' An Irish political advisor concurs, and illustrates how complicated things might be:

> *Would you say that you're a politician?*
> I think, while I might not admit it myself, I think it's certainly an accusation that would be levelled at me by my peers and most would say that I'm a politician to my fingertips. And probably they mean that in a type of cynical way, but I'm probably guilty in that regard. Yes.
> *What do you respond to them?*
> I laugh it off. It's very hard to plead innocent on that charge because all my adult life I've been active politically, so I mean it's pretty much in my DNA really.

Still other political advisors seem to have even greater difficulty deciding whether they are politicians or not, or they say that their perception of their role has changed over time. A political advisor in the Swedish government offices gets in a knot and states, 'I am a politician, so to speak, but I'm still not a politician but a political employee, a politically informed administrator.' A political secretary in the Swedish parliament also falters: 'I work for a politician and I have a political job but … well what is a "politician"?' Another political secretary in the Swedish parliament claims, '[I] was rather precise when I started here by having to say to people, "But I am an administrator, not a politician." Then that has become sort of blurred [laughs] with time.'

A parliamentary assistant in Ireland maintains that although people would *see* him as a politician, he would never *present* himself as one:

> *Do you see yourself as a politician?*
> Oh, I suppose I would. I clearly am. I'd be regarded as a politician, not an elected politician but I'd be regarded as a politician. /…/
> *Do you sometimes refer to yourself as a politician?*
> No, I never do. No, no. I would never do that, no, no.

The fact that we get several such slightly incoherent or diffuse answers from intelligent people is another indication of how diffuse the political role of policy professionals really is. And so is the fact that different policy professionals provide different answers to whether they are politicians or not.

Policy professionals who claim they are *not* politicians seem to focus mainly on the responsibility aspect of being a politician. Since they are not ultimately responsible for decisions and are not under the scrutiny of citizens and voters, they cannot be politicians. Policy professionals who claim that they *are* politicians (of sorts) instead focus on the influence aspect of their work. Since they have political influence and de facto wield political power, they are indeed politicians. The simple question about whether they are politicians or not therefore reveals some quite fundamental aspects of life as a policy professional.

If political advisors are divided on the issue of whether they are politicians or not, how do they perceive the elected politicians? Here again, a rather mixed response emerges. Many professionals express their admiration for the stamina and persistence of the leading politicians, like this press secretary in the Swedish government offices:

> (N)o matter what political colour a minister has, for example, they are really 'brutal' people. In a positive sense. They put all their engagement into this – remember what I said before about putting your personal life on hold. That is really the case. Work from six in the morning, at home by ten and then preparations for the next day, to bed at one, every day, all week long. The whole weekend they just have to sleep to catch up. /.../ You should be damned impressed by what they do; then they may have the wrong opinions, but let me put it this way: I am more impressed by how hard they work now than I was before.

The admiration for the leading politicians that many of their closest advisors express is tangible. As I will show in the next section, such admiration extends into deep loyalty to their masters and into a desire to serve and protect them. The possible democratic problems connected to the rise and extension of policy professionalism is hardly that policy professionals take a dim view of their closest politicians and circumvent or backstab them. Many political advisors express how deeply impressed they are by the hard work and dedication among their ministers or MPs.

However, when it comes to the *intellectual* capabilities of the *average* politician, many policy professionals are less impressed. A Swedish policy professional who at the time of the interview worked for a private firm but has a long experience at the core of politics states that 'most MPs are MPs because they cannot become local or regional mayors. That's the fact. Most MPs are not all that sharp.' A political secretary at the local level but with long experience with parliament shares this withering judgement. Certainly there were many MPs who were highly competent, but the great surprise was still 'that there were many who were of a very low quality', to the extent that one could wonder 'if they could even get a job outside politics if they tried'. A political advisor in the Irish government had equally low opinions on some of the TDs:

> And I think some of them just don't care. They know that they're going to get elected no matter what. There is no one there to challenge them. They're just biding time, doing what they have to do, just surviving.

In summary, policy professionals tend to have a rather mixed view of elected politicians. It could perhaps be said that policy professionals are typically very impressed by how hard politicians work, although some of them are seen as less diligent than others. They are typically less impressed by the analytical abilities of average politicians, although they think that some leading politicians are truly sharp, including in an intellectual sense. These distinctions between industriousness and intellectual acumen, and between 'the best and the rest', are further ingredients in the motivation package that make most policy professionals unwilling to enter the electoral arena. In all, policy professionals' views about the practices of representative democracy, including their judgement of the people who are selected in the processes, make most of them unwilling to go the electoral route themselves.

COMMITMENT AND LOYALTY

In spite of not being politicians, policy professionals are rarely 'guns for hire' that will work for any client and any purpose. They are typically deeply affected by loyalties and commitments that are important guiding forces in their work and careers. Virtually all policy professionals display a large degree of commitment to *the cause*. The cause may be found in the success for the broad political aims that one is attached to, but it could also be a cause committing to more specific issues, for example, gender equality or entrepreneurship. Broadly speaking, policy professionals are driven by ideologies and not primarily by detached expert knowledge.

The clearest statements about ideological commitments are probably found among policy professionals in trade unions and other interest organizations, since it is here that such commitment forms the strongest base for recruitment and motivation (see also Chapter 5). A research officer in a Swedish trade union explains:

> I have my roots in the working class. My parents were active in the union, had 'red' values. So I've grown up with a value commitment that I always had. /.../ And now when I work at [the trade union] I feel that I can work from the heart outwards. I have no problems adjusting what I say to my core values. So, in practice, I feel freer than ever to say what I think. Because I think very much like [the trade union] does. And I always did. I sort of always had this trade-union-friendly, 'red', ideological commitment.

What we see here is less a commitment to specific issues than a commitment to the broader cause of the working class and the labour movement. Such broad and deep commitment is found among many policy professionals; this commitment is most often what brought them into their line of business in the first place, and without it their work, in the long run, would be literally meaningless. This is why so few policy professionals would consider becoming a civil servant or some other public administrator; their ideological commitment would find no outlet in their daily work.

From the other end of the political spectrum, a former political advisor explains: 'I am deeply bourgeois and I believe in liberal and liberal-conservative values, but what engages me most of all is getting the right politics and the right policy.' Hence, ideological commitment is found at both ends of the political spectrum, and being driven by values is not the prerogative of any particular political inclination.

Even lobbyists and private consultants, who work for different clients, are often driven by their own commitments rather than those of their clients (Tyllström and Murray 2019). A Dutch communication advisor answers the question about whether she sees herself primarily as a commercial actor or as ideologically driven:

> Personally I'm ideologically driven.
> *How does that differ from being purely commercially driven?*
> It's because I'm constantly also thinking like, 'Do I agree with what I'm advising?' like, from a personal perspective. And that's sometimes hard because that's not your job. To give your personal opinion of course. But I think it can also … may produce better advice.

Private political consultants, communication advisors, lobbyists – however they may label themselves they are often seen by the rest of the policy professional world as devoid of ideological content, as slick operators working for any cause that will pay off. But this is hardly the case at the individual level. Lobbyists are most eager and ultimately successful when they lobby for causes they themselves believe in. And that is also why larger bureaus and agencies recruit employees from a broad political spectrum and then put their lobbyists to work on causes that align with their personal values and commitments. Smaller agencies instead try to choose their customers so they fit with what the agency itself feels are worthwhile causes.

Just as important as ideological commitments are loyalties of various kinds. Loyalty and commitment are of course tightly intertwined – one could even see ideological commitment as a particular form of loyalty, loyalty to a particular cause. But here I will reserve the term 'loyalty' for attachment to particular persons and organizations rather than broad ideological orientations.

Those policy professionals who work closely with leading politicians almost always express deep loyalty and personal admiration in relation to 'their' politician. An Irish political advisor in government expresses feelings that are shared by many others:

> The minister himself would be a role model from my point of view; I hugely admire the man. He's a man of great integrity, great honesty, and great values and ideals, and that's important. I think that if I didn't share those values I wouldn't have lasted the best part of 11 years working for him.

A second Irish political advisor concurs that working for her particular minister is what motivated her to take the job in the first place:

> I work with someone who is making [a difference] and I'm helping and working really closely together with somebody who is making huge changes in this country. She's phenomenal. What she has achieved in this country. /.../ For me it's almost a dream-come-true job to work for somebody like her.

With this loyalty comes a protective orientation towards the politician. Above all, nothing that the policy professional does should be allowed to harm the politician in any way. A Dutch political advisor explains why he was so hesitant about even granting me an interview:

> It's that unwritten rule that you do speak for him – but not too much and not too much in public. And then too, you have a kind of responsibility that what I say can be linked to my boss. You also, and I'm not sure if this is also the case in other countries, but one of the jobs is to protect and not expose him, and by saying a lot of stuff you're also exposing him.

This might be seen as one of the most important functions for political advisors and other policy professionals that work closely with politicians and other elected representatives. That they are there for them, no matter what, and that they serve as protectors, sounding boards, and therapeutic listeners. Politics is a hard, sometimes even vicious, game, and to stand it, you need someone to stand by your side, and to be someone in front of whom you can vent without being afraid that your rage will leak to the press.

Loyalties and commitments are also the basis for *value hierarchies* regarding jobs and positions. In particular, many policy professionals express reluctance to work for the PR industry. PR is a stigmatized line of work precisely because of a perceived lack of commitment, loyalty, and transparency: 'No one can really be held accountable because they are not responsible for the issues, but they charge a fee for conducting a mission and then they don't have any responsibility any longer.'

The stigmatization of PR and lobbying is also evident in the negative reactions some Swedish policy professionals express regarding (some aspects of) our previous book on policy professionals (Garsten, Rothstein, and Svallfors 2015). Some of the political advisors, research officers, and political directors feel clearly contaminated by being lumped together with the PR consultants under a common label. As put by a political director at a trade union:

> I don't feel like a threat to democracy. I am pretty open about what I do. I work on behalf of our members, I don't have any secret financiers. My financiers are membership fees. *Others have also talked about being lumped together with a whole profession ...* Yes, like KPMG or Kreab, who will not disclose their financiers or their clients and

blah blah blah. It is weird. I don't feel I'm there at all. I have no secret clients; we are completely transparent. I think these are different things. We are not a PR firm!

At the same time, we have seen that many PR consultants clearly express and enact an ideological commitment in their work. Many of them actively search for clients that may finance projects to which the consultants themselves are ideologically attached, and they are far from 'guns for hire' for any and all causes (Tyllström and Murray 2019). A Dutch lobbyist claims to be 'really idealistic' and to 'really enjoy working for /.../ an underdog' and to feel that if a client is 'aligned with your personal interest, then it's quite easy to work for them because it doesn't take a lot of energy, it brings more energy'.

An Irish lobbyist explains:

> I have put my hand up and said, 'I would give anything to work with this client. It would be massively important to me. I think they are brilliant.' I have even taken a cut in fees in order to win particular clients that I was particularly emotionally invested in, that I thought were brilliant clients that I wanted to work for.

Of course, sentiments such as these do not imply that political consultants and communication advisors typically work pro bono, or that payment does not matter for their commitment. It does mean, however, that many of them actually try to select customers for their causes and not the other way around (Tyllström and Murray 2019). They then become slightly offended when other policy professionals (and even professionals in their own line of business) see them simply as 'guns for hire' without any commitments beyond the bottom line.

In general, the degree of stigma that attaches to the lobbying industry seems to be inversely related to the 'maturity' of the lobbying market. In The Hague and Brussels, lobbying is everywhere and accepted as a natural state of affairs, while in the other three settings there is (still?) considerable suspicion surrounding lobbying and political consultancy. A Swedish lobbyist with experience from both Stockholm and Brussels expands on the difference in the status of lobbyists in the two settings:

> It is very different how a lobbying activity looks in Brussels compared to back home in Sweden. /.../ It is a little bit ugly in Sweden, to be a lobbyist; you are not a 'lobbyist' in Sweden, you call yourself something else. You are a 'communication consultant' or something like that. /.../ Here, it is really a *tool of the trade*. You are a lobbyist. What personal characteristics do you have that make you a good lobbyist? Why is he a successful lobbyist? Why is she not a successful lobbyist? It is a craft. You have to learn and know these things, and that is a refinement you can only get here in Brussels.

To sum up, ideological commitments and personal loyalties are fundamental aspects of policy professionalism. They are driving forces and motivating factors and they form the basis for value hierarchies among policy professionals. Being committed to the cause is of course very important for those who were recruited on an ideological base and are supposed to share their employers' values and ideology. But it is also important where it could be least expected: among the lobbyists and consultants that work for specific clients on specific contracts.

CONCLUSION: POWER WITHOUT RESPONSIBILITY

This chapter has been a story about the attractions of power without responsibility. Policy professionals are highly attracted by power, in its various forms and guises, but they shun visibility. Visibility in relation to voters, who can claim your time and attention and put you out of a job if they do not like what you do. Visibility in relation to mass media, where you want your message to be seen, but emphatically do not want to be seen yourself. Visibility makes you responsible in the eyes of the wider public, and policy professionals do not really want to be responsible or responsive. They want to be entrepreneurs in the field of political action, they want to invent and reinvent politics and policies. But they do not want the drudgery and personal exposure that comes with being ultimately responsible. And their views about the politicians who willingly expose themselves to such politics are quite mixed: admiration mixed with contempt, making a distinction between 'the best and the rest'.

At the core of political representation lies the relation between representative and represented (Manin 1997). The people we elect to office are supposed to be responsible for their actions and also to be responsive to their voters' wishes and intentions. This is not the typical policy professional way to relate to politics. Many of them abhor the thought of being responsible before and responsive to people who do not understand politics and policy making. The idea of having to convince people with little knowledge about and little interest in politics to support them is not something that typically fills the hearts of policy professionals with joy. This is also why many of them admire elected politicians, that they have the stamina to go on, relentlessly, in pursuit of voters and votes, and that they take the ultimate responsibility for what they say and do. But policy professionals typically do not want to shoulder that role themselves; their orientation is of a different kind.

What this adds up to is a quite different way to relate to politics and policy making than what is typically found among elected politicians or, for that matter, public administrators. In contrast to the 'representation-and-responsibility ethos' of elected politicians (Weber 1919 [1946]) and the 'public-interest ethos' of the civil service (Lundquist 1998), most political employees display a certain 'entrepreneurial ethos' in their political activities. The core value of the entrepreneurial ethos is *innovation*. In the political sphere this means coming up with new political ideas – big or small – and finding new ways to market and sell them in public debate and to voters (Svallfors 2017). Representation and responsibility are less central for the entrepreneurially oriented political actors, who prefer to work behind the scenes and who do not want to be judged by uninformed publics. I will return to this in the concluding chapter.

While the attractions of power without responsibility are common for most policy professionals, the reasons why they prefer their way of doing politics to the elected variant differ among national contexts. The slow and boring nature of political careers combined with relentless media pressure (Sweden), the raw, uneducated, and unseemly aspects of politics (Latvia), the tyranny of localism (Ireland), and the hollow and personalized politics in a consensus-driven polity (the Netherlands) are four variants of the unbearable aspects many policy professionals find in elected politics. Each political system seems to produce its own discontent when it comes to reaching and upholding elected office, and most policy professionals are happy about not having to endure it.

Despite their shunning of elected politics and their sometimes scathing views about politicians, it is still important not to paint policy professionals as engaged in any kind of behind-the-back machinations against their elected leaders. Policy professionals often display a deep personal admiration for the political and organizational leaders they are supposed to serve, and they tend to share their value commitments and political strivings. Nor should they be described as 'guns for hire', applying their political expertise in the service of anyone able and willing to pay. Policy professionals are typically driven by political passions, ideological commitment, and loyalties. They are emphatically neither impartial administrators nor dispassionate truth-seeking academics, but political and ideological animals.

And yet there is something slightly disturbing about policy professionals' unwillingness to take full responsibility for their actions. It allows them the luxury of exercising power without catching the blame if things go wrong (Garsten, Rothstein, and Svallfors 2015: 218–25). This might in fact be seen as one of the big advantages for those who exert political power in the policy professional mode.

The *dis*advantage with this stealth mode of operation is that policy professionals can rarely claim full credit for the good deeds and smart things they do. But this is of little concern to most policy professionals, like one Irish political advisor who answers the question 'Who do you most of all want recognition and praise from when you have done something that is good?' with 'I don't; I want my boss to get recognition.' Many policy professionals actually seem to share the attitude of Henry VIII's 16th century advisor Thomas Cromwell that author Hilary Mantel portrays in one of her novels: 'Henry wants to be told he is behaving well, in the sight of God and man. "Cromwell," he says, "you know what we should try? Cromwell, would it not reflect well on my honour if I ...? Cromwell, would it not confound my enemies if ...?" And all these are the ideas you put to him last week. Never mind. You don't want the credit. You just want action.'[3]

NOTES

1. Peter Mair, 'We Must Move from Regarding State as Enemy and Oppressor', https://www.irishtimes.com/opinion/we-must-move-from-regarding-state-as-enemy-and-oppressor-1.602538 (accessed 10 July 2019).
2. These figures build on information on the websites of respective (lower level chamber of) parliaments, complemented with web searches (LinkedIn, etc.). The included parliamentary bodies are *Riksdagen* in Sweden, *Tweedekamer* in the Netherlands, *Saeima* in Latvia, and *Dáil Éireann* in Ireland. The reported figures build on all MPs in each country. If only MPs where full CVs can be obtained are included, numbers are still 40 per cent for the Netherlands, but rise to 38 per cent in Latvia, 29 per cent in Sweden, and 17 per cent in Ireland.
3. Quoted from Hilary Mantel, *Bring Up the Bodies*. London: HarperCollins, 2013, p. 248.

REFERENCES

Caro, Robert 1982–2012. *The Years of Lyndon Johnson (4 Vols)*. New York: Alfred A. Knopf.
Collins, Neil, and Mary O'Shea. 2003. 'Clientilism: Facilitating Rights and Favours.' In *Public Administration and Public Policy in Ireland: Theory and Methods*, edited by Maura Adshead and Michelle Millar, pp. 88–107. London: Routledge.
Garsten, Christina, Bo Rothstein, and Stefan Svallfors. 2015. *Makt utan mandat. De policyprofessionella i svensk politik*. Stockholm: Dialogos.
Lijphart, Arend. 1968. *The Politics of Accommodation: Pluralism and Democracy in the Netherlands*. Berkeley, CA: University of California Press.
Lundquist, Lennart. 1998. *Demokratins väktare: ämbetsmännen och vårt offentliga etos*. Lund: Studentlitteratur.
Manin, Bernhard. 1997. *The Principles of Representative Government*. New York: Cambridge University Press.
Pridham, Geoffrey. 2017. 'Post-Soviet Latvia: A Consolidated Democracy in the Third Decade of Independence?' In *Latvia – A Work in Progress? 100 Years of State- and Nationbuilding*, edited by David J Smith, pp. 189–203. Stuttgart: Ibidem-Verlag.
Svallfors, Stefan. 2017. 'Knowing the Game: Motivations and Skills among Policy Professionals.' *Journal of Professions and Organization* 4 (1): 55–69, doi: https://doi.org/10.1093/jpo/jow008.
Tyllström, Anna, and John Murray. 2019. 'Lobbying the Client? The Role of Hired Lobbyists in Corporate Political Activity.' *Organization Studies* Advance access.
Weber, Max. 1919. 'Politics as Vocation.' Reprinted in 1946, *From Max Weber: Essays in Sociology*, edited by Hans H. Gerth and C. Wright Mills, pp. 77–128. New York: Oxford University Press.

5.   The peculiar market for political skills

with Niels Selling[1]

In the remake of the political drama series *House of Cards*, we find Senator Frank Underwood (played by Kevin Spacey) coolly complaining about Remy Danton, a former staffer turned lobbyist:

> Such a waste of talent. He chose money over power. In this town, a mistake nearly everyone makes. Money is the McMansion in Sarasota that starts falling apart after 10 years. Power is the old stone building that stands for centuries. I cannot respect someone who doesn't see the difference.

Most policy professionals would understand exactly what Senator Underwood was talking about. Their careers span many different organizational positions and sometimes they concern transitions from government to lobbying. But do they actually choose money over power in their career choices? As will be shown in this chapter, the particular skills policy professionals have acquired on their jobs is the currency that most affects their careers. But regarding their career motives and considerations, a less clear-cut picture than the one Frank Underwood paints will transpire.

In many democratic societies, what has emerged in the course of the last few decades is a labour market, where political skills are bought and sold. Politics is indeed for hire, not in the sense that every policy professional will work for any and all purposes that someone will pay for, but in the sense that skilled professionals move in the political field between different organizations that hire them for short- or long-term missions. The boundary-spanning nature of policy professionals is visible not only in their day-to-day activities but also, and perhaps primarily, in their careers, as they frequently move between organizations whose intent it is to affect politics and policy making.

In the political labour market, people circulate between different positions where there is a demand for their particular skills, creating networks that span organizational boundaries. A Swedish political advisor in the European Parliament relates how a re-entering Member of the European Parliament (MEP) discovered that something new had emerged on the scene:

> So when [the MEP] came in now in [the last election] [the MEP] discovered that there was this brand new subculture that hadn't even existed 20 years earlier. Now

there were scores of people, as [the MEP] described it to me later, who had their primary relations to people in the other parties who did the same thing, or at PR agencies. We used to be a part of the party apparatus, and the ombudsmen and the members were far more important than people in the other parties, but this was a subculture of people who moved in the same bars and so on. Some were bragging about how much influence they had, while others were more low-key, but it was completely accepted this thing with people floating between PR agencies, party offices, the mayors' offices, and so on, and [the MEP] was completely shocked by this.

From the other end of the bargain, things look considerably less shocking, as coolly explained by this Swedish lobbyist in Brussels:

> Many of us who are policy professionals stick to our last, so to speak. Because even if people do not believe it, it is actually an occupation, and you can be more or less skilled in an occupation, and many of us know this thing properly. So then we get picked by either private companies, organizations or public affairs firms, so it is more individual what you feel for and what you want to do for the moment.

The policy professionals' skills that we have made acquaintance with in the previous chapters are marketable in this new expanding labour market. In this chapter, we will look more closely at this labour market and the careers of policy professionals, or more specifically, at the factors and considerations that guide their career decisions and opportunities. We will ask what specifically is for sale in their labour market, what the buyers and sellers in this market offer each other, and what prompts decisions to stay in, move within, or exit from this labour market.

Previous research on policy professionals' careers and labour market has mainly paid attention to the 'revolving door' between government/parliament and lobbying (Blanes i Vidal, Draca, and Fons-Rosen 2012, Parker 2009, Parker, Parker, and Dabros 2012, Tyllström 2019). In this literature, 'revolvers' are mainly seen as driven by financial considerations. Politics is the arena where certain skills and valuable contacts are acquired. These skills and networks can then be sold and transformed into economic gains. But since networks expire and skills devaluate, 'revolvers' need repeated stints in politics to retain their market value. Consequently, they come across as quite similar to other temporarily hired skilled professionals who rotate into and out of various organizations and in doing so accumulate marketable experience (Barley and Kunda 2004).

However, the policy professional labour market includes many other transitions and trajectories besides the 'revolving door'. Policy professionals may move from parliament to government as their party enters a government coalition, or back again after an election is lost. Think-tankers may become political consultants, and business association experts may become contract lobbyists.

Many moves are possible in policy professional careers and it is the intention in this chapter to map and illuminate how this broader labour market works. Through this analysis we understand what constitutes policy professionalism as a field – a field that spans various organizations and organizational types.

In doing so, we will move beyond the simple condemnation of people who move from politics to lobbying or vice versa that is often found in the public debate. We will rather try to formulate the specific labour market problems that policy professionals are exposed to and that sometimes prompt them to make choices with less than fortunate democratic implications. We will show how the combinations of skill possessions, values, and commitment shape the choices and trajectories of policy professional careers.

The chapter starts by describing the particular labour market dilemma that policy professionals find themselves in – their 'golden cage' – because of the particular character of their skills and resources. The chapter then delves into the role played by considerations about power in the policy professional careers, their actual trajectories across a six-year span, and their perceived career opportunities and constraints. This part of the chapter builds primarily on a career analysis on Swedish data over a five-year period. The chapter concludes with some observations regarding the wider implications of the findings in the chapter.

THE GOLDEN CAGE

To begin, we need to properly understand the labour market situation of policy professionals: they are skilled professionals who know about complex and partly hidden processes and can apply such knowledge in order to achieve their organizations' aims and strategies. Such skills are useful and in demand in the labour market, but only in a particular niche. For recruitment into many professional occupations the specific on-the-job acquired skills of policy professionals are hard to evaluate since these professionals have no special licence or formal credentials to show what they know and can do. At the same time, in their particular niche of the labour market their skills are in high demand across many different employing organizations.

When policy professionals ponder over their career opportunities, many of them – and this goes in particular for those who work in the government offices and for political parties – identify exactly this specific career problem: that the political knowledge they have is so hard to evaluate. It may be hard for many private companies, public agencies, and other prospective employers to understand and correctly value what, for example, a few years in the government offices really entail. A Swedish political secretary in parliament with previous experience from the government offices explains that there 'are few who know what the job contains, it's hard to explain what the job contains, it's hard to explain what competence one has, and so on. /.../ It becomes a sort of validation problem quite simply.'

A political advisor in the Swedish government offices agrees that it is hard to explain what you really know when you apply for other positions. You know 'a lot of stuff that surely could be useful in other places, but I realized when I was looking for jobs that it wasn't all that easy to explain what I know – explain what I know so that it becomes useful for someone else'. A parliamentary assistant in Ireland summarizes: 'There is no real correlation between a parliamentary assistant and any other job. Really. Your skills are quite unique. And I don't mean "unique." It's not transferable.'

A young political advisor in the Dutch government offices notices that 'People outside don't have a clue about what this job means,' and complains in a rather touching way about misunderstandings about what his job entails:

> For example, they hear 'political assistant' and then they can always read it as 'ah, he was the one who was always there and did his agenda, did his e-mail and ...', so you first have to explain that that was not what you were doing.
> *They see you as some kind of secretary in a sense?*
> And my age doesn't help as well. Because they think that 'you're so young, you cannot have done anything that has substance because you're way too young to have done that'. So that doesn't help either.
> *So how do you solve that situation?*
> I don't know. Do you know how to solve it?

The fact that this political advisor turns to me as the interviewer for advice on how to solve his career problems is a further indication of how problematic many policy professionals find the fact that their skills are hard to evaluate properly.

Hence, it may be hard to get employment that corresponds with the policy professional's true abilities. Doors are shut just because the employing organization cannot valuate what they really know, all the useful insights they have acquired in politics. A Swedish policy professional in a private company states that when employment is sought in private businesses one often encounters questions that indicate scepticism: 'What have you done then? Well, you have worked in the government offices, in parliament, for an employer organization or a trade union. And what are we to do with that knowledge?' Such problems become particularly acute when elections are lost, and many former political advisors and other policy professionals connected to parties have to look for other jobs:

> I don't think many people know what this work and what this job entails. /.../ So with our party losing as much, we had a lot of good policy advisors and state secretaries that found it quite difficult to get a new job. (Political advisor, Dutch government)

Both policy professionals and elected politicians therefore face a 'golden cage' problem. It is 'golden' to the extent that it offers considerable attractions for people interested in politics and policy making, but it is a 'cage' to the extent that the skills you acquire in the job are fungible only across a fairly narrow segment of the labour market. As put by a Swedish policy professional working for a private company but with long-standing experience from public offices:

> Most political employees and politicians are trapped in a golden cage. That is to say, they have rather good remuneration. Maybe they make fifty thousand per month. They do what they basically have done since they were teenagers /.../ Work opportunities outside politics for these people are very limited unless they choose to do conscious career planning from the very beginning. So they become serfs in a sense, and many of them are unhappy because they want to try something different but they never get invited to start anywhere.

It is at this point that a particular form of private company – the PR agencies (or public affairs agencies or communication consultancies, or lobbying firms – these firms go by different names) – becomes central in the careers of many policy professionals. These enterprises know how to appreciate and value policy professionals' know-how, so they act as political capital exchanges. In contrast to most other private firms, PR agencies can fully appreciate and value the political know-how of the policy professionals, since this is the main commodity that they offer to their customers, and since the industry already contains many ex-politicians and ex-political advisors. As put by a political advisor in the Dutch parliament:

> There are quite a lot of big lobby bureaus, so if you go into those sectors then of course they know a bit about what you've done, and that's an advantage because you know the rules and … but if you go a bit further outside of that I think it's really hard to explain what you do.

For this Swedish political advisor, the PR agencies can even be seen as saviours:

> As soon as I think about the future, I get such anxiety because I have to finish my education. So I don't really know. But of course a natural step forward that many take is through the PR industry and then onwards. And I suppose I haven't closed that door completely. And that step, it often comes because that is one of very few branches where political merits can be validated into something else. /.../ If an employer is about to hire someone and it says 'MP' or 'Political advisor in the Government Offices' on the CV, very few know what that means and understand how it may be transformed into something that is useful for the business. But the PR business, it is said, is the validation tool where political [advisors] can use their knowledge about how things work but also their personal networks and creativity. And to get into private business.

The lobbying and communication advice industry can in this way work as a stepping stone to other parts of the private sector. Policy professionals can show their abilities in a marketized line of work where at the same time they can use everything they have learned in politics. Once they have shown themselves useful in a profit-oriented industry they also become employable in many other parts of the private sector as communication and policy experts. In this way, the lobbying and communication advice firms work as 'bridges' to overcome institutional buffers that hinder the flow of information, 'a line in a network which provides the only path between two points', as put by sociologist Mark Granovetter in his famous analysis of the importance of 'weak ties' (Granovetter 1973: 1364). In this case, such firms provide one of the few clear-cut links between the world of politics and the world of business.

There is no doubt that these firms actively search for people with broad political experience, and they aim to recruit from a broad political spectrum. Their main interest is not the personal networks of political employees, even though, of course, a well-filled address book is a resource. It is, rather, detailed knowledge about politics and policy making, about when and where it is possible to have some influence, that they look for. As put by a recruiter at such a firm, they look for people who can 'understand the political game and this informal [part]' that forms the political content, someone who has the right 'gut feeling' for what is happening and has happened in politics.

For this young Swedish political consultant on the way into politics, this stepping stone is seen as very useful in the future career:

> I will raise my value considerably. I see this as a way to improve my negotiation position in order to get a better job, higher salary, new work tasks. I will have contacts in politics. That is a very strong currency in the world of consulting. So to have experience of how a political organization works, have contacts there, know political communication, opinion-formation in that way, is something that is sought after. And then I will be able to work much more with that kind of communication work too, even if I go back to consulting later.

The recruiters at the firms confirm that such interchanges between politics and their industry are seen as valuable. One Swedish recruiter states that the agency directly encourages such movements into and out of party politics: 'If you come back later, you are most often a much better advisor.'

So the problem of evaluating skills can find a solution in the activities of the PR sector (even if far from all policy professionals would ever consider working in this sector, see Chapter 4 and the rest of this chapter). But there are further aspects of the golden cage problem. One, as was discussed in Chapter 3, is that policy professionals are very dependent on their local networks and local information. This means there is very little in the way of an international labour market for policy professionals. They can rarely move between local contexts in the way, for example, academics, computer specialists, or chemical engineers can do quite easily.

In our sample, this fact is articulated most clearly by Swedish policy professionals working as lobbyists or political advisors in Brussels. Swedish policy professionals almost to a person complain that what they do in Brussels is so invisible to prospective employers in Stockholm that they fear that their merits would count for little if they tried to get back to Sweden at some point in their career: 'I think we are quite bad in Sweden to appreciate, to understand, what it means, what merits you have got, and experiences /.../ and this is grounded in the fact that you do not really know how it works, what you really do at the Commission and what that implies, and there are many myths about the jobs here,' explains a policy advisor for a trade union. Furthermore, local networks in Stockholm have expired if and when the time comes for returning to Sweden, as explained by this political advisor in the European Parliament:

> *But is a time in Brussels a merit, do you think, when you come back to Stockholm?*
> That's not evident, I think.
> *Why not?*
> Because perhaps you are not known enough. You could, for example, look at those who have worked as party political [employees] and then go to Brussels – they get a little forgotten. So once you come back it's like 'Ok, but what have you done lately?' There is this gap between the EU and national politics.

This gap between Stockholm and Brussels is also evidenced by the fact that almost no policy professionals in Stockholm mention the European Commission, the European Parliament, or the Brussels lobbying scene when asked about future career prospects and dreams (Garsten, Rothstein, and Svallfors 2015: 134). They are simply too dependent on their local information and local networks to consider a career transition to Brussels. Instead, being a policy professional at the EU level requires specific knowledge about the EU institutions and specific networks connected to that political machinery (Büttner et al. 2015, Georgakakis and Rowell 2013, Laurens 2018).

It is quite possible that this disconnect between the national and EU levels is smaller in a country such as the Netherlands, which is much physically closer to Brussels, and where lobbying, just as in Brussels, is more long-standing and legitimate. On the other hand, The Hague and Brussels are still two different worlds in terms of networks and information, so perhaps Dutch policy professionals in Brussels find their career prospects just as locally circumscribed as the Swedes do. In our data we cannot establish which of the scenarios is more accurate since only Swedish policy professionals were interviewed in Brussels. But we do note that hardly any policy professionals in any of the countries mention the EU scene in Brussels as a likely or desirable destination.

If the specificity of their skills, which makes them hard to evaluate, is one career problem that policy professionals face, and the dependency on local contexts is another, there is a third and perhaps more subtle aspect of the golden cage problem. That is that for many or perhaps most policy professionals, it is hard to think about a future career outside the buzzing, whirling, conflict-ridden – in a word, exciting – world of politics in the broad sense. As a Dutch advisor at a political party pondering his future career put it: 'The problem is that once you've started working in politics where there are always disputes, lots of other jobs you are looking at look so *dull*.'

This is the main reason why relatively few policy professionals would consider a future career in the civil service or other parts of the public administration, even when their skills may be attractive to such employers. They find a non-political and non-committed role too circumscribed, too devoid of excitement, too timid. 'No, no, no, I just couldn't' is the unequivocal answer of an Irish think-tanker when asked about going into civil service, 'I feel politically constrained *here* – what would I feel in civil service?' A political director at a Swedish trade union concurs:

> I am really not a civil servant; I mean the irreproachable public administrator is far from what I am even though I am not corrupt or anything like that. I am value driven and that is not what the irreproachable public administrator should be in the same way.

Hence, policy professionals are both attractive in their particular labour market niche and quite circumscribed regarding which positions they can or want to aim for. Theirs is a particular golden cage, in which their skills are fungible across a broad set of organizations and in which there is excitement to be found. But moving outside the golden cage is restricted by the incommensurability of their skills, by their dependence on local information and networks, and by their own desire to stay where values matter and occupational life is exciting.

TRAJECTORIES IN THE FIELD

Although Swedish policy professionals rarely transfer between the national and the EU levels, they move quite a lot between various organizations at the national level. In this and the following sections we will delve into how Swedish policy professionals' careers have evolved over a six-year period from 2012 to 2018.

In this analysis, we discern six types of organizations in the policy professional field: (1) Government offices; (2) Parliamentary parties; (3) Trade unions; (4) Other major interest organizations; (5) Think tanks; (6) PR firms.

A comprehensive mapping of these organizations, in 2012, gave a total of 913 individuals occupying positions that were non-elected and yet both partisan and policy relevant.[2] We quantitatively mapped the work trajectories of these 913 policy professionals between 2012 and 2018, resulting in 788 complete career descriptions (most of the missing data can be attributed to retirements).[3]

Table 5.1 displays career moves among these different organizational types. To simplify, the table only includes positions in 2012 and 2018, while any intermediary career steps are disregarded.

As shown in the table, policy professionals frequently move across different types of organizations, but there is also a large share that remains within the same organizational type. No one remains as a policy professional in the government offices due to the fact that political advisors go when their minister goes, and since the government changed hands in 2014 there was a complete overhaul of the political staff. The largest share remaining within the same organizational type is instead found among trade unions and other interest organizations, where about two-thirds remain in the same organizational type.

We also observe certain outflows that are less likely than others. There is little movement between trade unions and other interest organizations (a majority of which are associated with business interests) and between trade unions and PR firms.

We also find that very few policy professionals become politicians, which confirms their expressed reluctance to move into elected positions (see Chapter 4). Instead, the most common destinations outside the policy professional field are private companies (other than PR firms) and public administration, including civil service positions.

In Table 5.2, we summarize how many in 2018 *remain* in the same organization they were in as of 2012, how many have *moved* to other organizations of the same or different organizational types, and how many have *exited* from the policy professional field.

As shown in Table 5.2, there is considerable flux in the field when we look at the specific organizations people work for in 2018 compared to 2012. Rather consistently across all organizational types (except for the government) there is an almost even split between those who are attached to the same employer and those who have moved on to other organizations. PR consultants appear most mobile – 60 per cent have left the organization for which they worked in 2012 – while policy professionals in trade unions and other major interest organizations exhibit the strongest tendency to remain.

The table also shows that no one has moved between different political parties, and hardly anyone has moved between two think tanks. In addition to what is found in the table, our data reveal that only one person has switched between the main employers' federation (*Svenskt näringsliv*) and either of the two main trade unions (*LO* and *TCO*) or their constituent member organiza-

Table 5.1   Movements between organizational types 2012–18 (no in-betweens)

2012 \ 2018	Government (%)	Parliament (%)	Trade unions (%)	Interest organizations (%)	PR firms (%)	Think tanks (%)	Other (PP, %)	Public administration (%)	Private company (%)	Politician (%)	Other (not PP) (%)	Total
Government	0	7	3	21	12	3	4	22	22	4	1	143
Parliament	14	44	4	7	7	0	5	6	7	4	1	163
Trade unions	4	4	67	5	1	3	1	10	4	0	0	141
Interest organizations	1	1	1	66	7	1	2	5	12	2	2	131
PR firms	1	4	1	8	56	0	3	4	20	1	1	157
Think tanks	4	6	2	9	7	56	0	4	7	0	6	54

Politics for hire

Table 5.2   Remain, move, exit 2012–18

	Remain within organization (%)	Move within organizational type (%)	Move outside organizational type (%)	Exit (%)
Government	0	0	55	45
Parliament	44	0	39	17
Trade unions	55	12	21	13
Interest organizations	50	16	14	21
PR firms	40	16	19	25
Think tanks	52	4	31	13
Total	39	8	30	23

tions. Furthermore, no one has ever moved from a think tank affiliated with the political left to one affiliated with the political right, or vice versa. This indicates that there are ideological barriers for moves within the field, something to which we will return later in the chapter.

Table 5.2 also displays the propensity of policy professionals to exit from the field. This varies markedly across categories. Policy professionals from the government offices, interest organizations, and PR firms are most prone to exit (with private companies as the most common destination). It is interesting to observe that governmental political appointees, who belong to the innermost circles of power, are most likely to exit from the field.[4] People working for trade unions, political parties, or think tanks are less likely to do so.

The flux in the policy professional labour market indicates that the skills of these professionals are largely transferable between different types of organizations. However, there might be barriers other than ideology, namely, limitations on the kinds of positions attainable from different kinds of origins. To test this, Table 5.3 shows all movements between three broad functions among policy professionals: managers, policy officers, and communicators.[5] In contrast to Tables 5.1 and 5.2, Table 5.3 includes all job changes between 2012 and 2018 in order to show which transitions are more likely than others. The upper panel includes all job changes, while the lower panel excludes changes to or from PR firms, which in the upper panel have all been classified as 'communication'. Although their categorization as 'communication' is probably adequate in most cases, their job may still include some policy proposal work, depending on the specific mission and person.

We find in Table 5.3 that almost two-thirds of job shifts from communication functions go to other communication functions, while about half of the job shifts from policy functions go to other policy functions. Managers' job changes are more evenly spread between functions, even though the

Table 5.3   *Movements between positions 2012–18*

		All movements			
To	Manager (%)	Policy (%)	Communication (%)	Other (%)	Total
From					
Manager	34	20	33	13	139
Policy	14	46	29	11	336
Communication	13	13	65	8	381
Other	12	18	27	42	33
		All movements excluding PR			
To	Manager (%)	Policy (%)	Communication (%)	Other (%)	Total
From					
Manager	39	26	17	19	96
Policy	15	51	22	12	304
Communication	11	18	62	9	197
Other	13	19	25	44	32

most common job shift is to another management position. So, in summary, results from Table 5.3 suggest that there are also certain skill barriers in the policy professional labour market; these especially pertain to communication functions, which seem to be somewhat specialized and hence subject to within-function job shifts.

For the other three countries – Ireland, Latvia, and the Netherlands – we have no comparable data. However, some crude indicators may be found in a mapping of how many of the interviewees have left for other positions within a two-year period 2017–19. We find that one-third of the interviewees have changed positions within this short time frame. Not one of them has become an MP or a government minister, a handful have gone from parliamentary or government offices to PR, and a couple have gone into public administration. No one has moved from PR to other organizational types, but a couple have shifted between different PR agencies. All in all, as far as can be judged from such rudimentary data, there is nothing to indicate that the Swedish patterns are highly distinct for that particular country, but we could suspect that patterns might be fairly similar had we been able to conduct a more thorough analysis also for other countries.

POWER OVER MONEY

We now move to an analysis of the considerations and motivations behind career decisions and outcomes, based on interview data from Sweden. Between 2012 and 2013, a total of 71 Swedish policy professionals, selected on the basis of position, gender, age, and political party affiliation, were interviewed. We used a semi-structured interview format covering key aspects of their work and careers. A subsample of the interviewees from this first round were re-interviewed in 2018 (N = 32). These interviews were again semi-structured, but this time the focus was on the interviewees' careers since 2012 and their considerations in this regard. The selection of re-interviewees was strategic in order to cover those who had *remained* in the same job since 2012, those who had *moved* to other policy professional positions in the field, and those who had *exited* from the policy professional field. [6]

The whole field that policy professionals inhabit is imbued with political power, and previous chapters have shown that the desire to affect politics – and society at large – is the prime motivating force among policy professionals. It is therefore to be expected that power would be a key concern for them when deciding whether to remain or move. But a closer look at exactly how power motivates career decisions reveals a less obvious picture. In a previous chapter we discerned three different aspects of power, each of which is important for motivating policy professionals in their daily work, but also for driving their career decisions and moves. What is 'up' and what is 'down' in terms of career is decided by access to power, in its various guises and aspects.

One such aspect is power as *agency*, the ability to affect decisions and outcomes. Here we find that what often motivates moves from one policy professional position to another is either a prospective power gain in a new position or an actual power loss in the previous position. But considerations about power as agency can also lie behind the decision to stay in a position because it offers power that cannot be matched elsewhere.

A research officer in a trade union is clear that the decision to stay in the current position is based on the fact that 'your influence grows because you get more experience-based knowledge. You know what buttons to push, you know which politician to approach, you know which committee you should target to influence politics.'

In a similar vein, someone at the other end of the political spectrum explains the decision to move from PR to an interest organization as a way to increase power as agency:

> If you are interested in public opinion, if you are interested in social issues, if you have a political background, and a political outlook that tilts toward the liberal spectrum, as I have, and think that questions about market economy and entrepre-

neurship and open borders and integration through work are important and so on, then it's hard to say no to doing this at an organization that above all has a very long time perspective, and also some muscle and some resources.

Yet another person explains why leaving a trade union office for public administration made sense:

> They reorganized, so the unit that I was responsible for – policy, politics, opinion, and influence – was incorporated into our huge negotiation department and got a somewhat different role, not as independent and not as much focused on public opinion /.../ They moved the research to the negotiation department and then they moved the PR bit itself to communication and then you lost some of the things we had been building for some years and that I was a part of.

The loss of power can sometimes, in a slightly paradoxical way, be the result of success for one's own political party. Once your own party gets into government, working in the parliament becomes less attractive since the important action will take place in the government offices. This political secretary explains why winning an election would be a reason for leaving parliament:

> I wouldn't like to stay in the parliamentary office if we were in government. That is super boring. I have a hard time seeing that there would be anything there that I would think was fun. You become very much a marketing department, and that bit I don't think is fun.

The second aspect is power as *proximity*, being close to power and to the spaces and circles where important decisions are made. Many policy professionals who have experienced the buzzing, whirling world that is the government offices speak longingly about one day returning there, if elections go well and someone asks them to step in. 'It is this tempo and speed that I know almost everybody who left misses' muses one former political advisor, and a second advisor agrees:

> You have the information before anyone else has. It boosts your ego somehow. I know what will be in the newspaper tomorrow, I have the answer to all that is speculated about, I am here in this car with the minister who is responsible for this, the person everyone looks for and everybody wants to get hold of, and I know how she reasons, and with my limited competence and experience I can still talk to this person about it. That part is what you miss I suppose, that it boosts your ego, it is 'wow', and you can have first-hand insight in a way I no longer have.

Given half a chance, many policy professionals who have left the government offices would soon return there. But even if the government offices offer the strongest attraction of proximity to power, many other policy professionals in other positions enjoy being in circles and rooms where important decisions are made, where important people show up, where you know stuff before anyone else does.

The third aspect is power as *self-determination*; being able to define one's own work and expressions is an important determinant for decisions about staying in or leaving a particular position. As explained by this former political advisor who now works at an interest organization: 'In the position I have, I have to do what I believe in myself. /.../ So I have a great deal of freedom to act according to what I find right and reasonable.'

Power as self-determination often implies a trade-off with power as agency. In the circles closest to power, it is often hard to achieve self-determination, as the advisor continues:

> You cannot set your own calendar, you cannot steer your own thoughts, but you must stay within a given frame and you often have to push issues, or at least it happens that you have to push issues that you definitely don't like.

Since power is so central to the policy professionals' motivations, hardly anyone admits to having actually lost power through their choices or forced circumstances. They are helped by the fact that various aspects of power may substitute for others, for example, losing proximity to power can be coun-terbalanced by gaining more self-determination. Furthermore, having strong personal influence in a less powerful organization may be substituted for less personal influence but in an organization that wields substantial power. This reluctance to admit a loss of power is a further indication of how important power is for the careers of policy professionals.

The lure of power is modified by policy professionals' need to find personal financial security in their volatile labour market. Although many of them are adamant that salary is not an important factor in their decisions about career moves, others point to the need for, and problems with finding, future employment as one important consideration behind their career decisions. Furthermore, most would be unhappy to be paid less in a new position com-pared to the one they left.

The ambivalent attitude towards pay is clearly articulated in this description of a salary negotiation in the Swedish government offices:

> They always have to ask what salary you want, and then I had 35k, and I wanted 45k, and she was like 'That is a 10k raise', and I was like 'Yeah ...', and then she started to babble on about how I should think about those who were the same age

as me and worked at the party headquarters with the web and so on and that they would be envious. /.../
But what if she had said 'No, 35k, you don't get anything more,' would you then have gone home and complained a bit and then still accepted it?
Yes.
You would have?
I would have, yes.

For most policy professionals, power is much more important than money, and some of them even left much better-paid positions in private companies to be able to wield influence. At the same time, bills need to get paid, and some stress the uncertainty of their positions and the need to find employment before their skills start to depreciate, as explained by a former political advisor:

> Immediately I guess I felt a small nagging worry. Had I been completely unaffected by that, I don't think I would have taken [the last job], but you never know. Your human capital degenerates, after all. You wouldn't be able to be on leave for two years and then get a decent job. Actually.

This is also a consequence of the fact that people get accustomed to certain lifestyles and may be reluctant to compromise these, even if money is not the most important consideration.

So in sum, power in its various guises is the most important motivation behind policy professionals' career decisions, even if this is tempered by motivations related to material rewards and security. But often, no strong trade-off has to be made since the most powerful positions also tend to be comparatively well paid.

AVENUES, BARRIERS, AND EXITS

What makes policy professionals employable in a large variety of organizations is the set of skills, described in a previous chapter, that provides them with knowledge of the political system. This knowledge is hard to acquire anywhere other than in policy-related positions, and it has limited marketability outside the policy professional sphere, mostly confined to the public affairs divisions of large companies and, to a smaller extent, various public agencies (Allern 2011, Svallfors 2016). But in the policy professional labour market, these skills are quite fungible across a variety of organizations and positions (Parker 2009).

The fungibility of their political skills could in principle result in career patterns that stretch equally across all kinds of positions and organizations. Still, as we showed in Tables 5.1–5.3, some career moves are far less common than others. What are the barriers in the labour market that lie behind these patterns? One such barrier could be related to the kinds of skills different policy professionals have.

The quantitative analysis revealed that two-thirds of the switches from communication led to other positions in communication, while half of those who worked with policy moved on to other policy functions. Is this indicative of two largely separate career tracks and, if so, what is the underlying reason? A political advisor in the government offices describes considerations about the next job:

> Should I confess that it is communication I am good at and seek jobs as a communication strategist and head of communication, with the risk of getting stuck there, or should I try to branch out into policy or something where I can work with analysis? The risk is that you end up in the communication fold. For example, it is very rare that the chief of communication [for a party] becomes a government minister, because you become part of the 'those-who-just-deal-with-the-surface gang' instead of those who deal with content.

While a skill barrier might somewhat separate communication from policy, many interviewees acknowledge that a policy professional needs to be good at both and that their future careers are not limited to one or the other. Rather, it is the preference for one over the other that constitutes the barrier. As put by a former political advisor who used to work with communication:

> A totally central aspect of Swedish politics, or politics in general, is to be able to formulate yourself in a way that is punchy and helps your superiors to communicate their message in punchy ways. I wish I didn't have to do that. /.../ I don't want to become a communication advisor, and I don't see myself as a communication advisor. /.../ I don't think the work tasks are as interesting. They do not reach the same level of originality, and the career tracks are less interesting.

Hence, the decision to work in analysis or communication very much comes down to personal preferences and taste. Policy professional careers can quite easily shift from one track to the other in this regard, since they all need to have a little of both skills to function in their occupational role.

But there are other barriers in their labour market which are less easy to transcend. The ideological commitment as a career determinant has already been discussed in the quantitative analysis. Since a certain political outlook is usually what brought policy professionals into their line of work in the first place (see Chapter 4), it is no surprise that this commitment features prominently in their later career decisions.

As pointed out in the previous chapter, ideological commitment is tightly linked to various types of loyalties. Here we may make a distinction between loyalty to specific persons and loyalty to specific parties or organizations. As we found in Chapter 4, many policy professionals in the government and party offices voice a strong personal loyalty to 'their' leading politician, as expressed by this former advisor: 'I work for [this particular minister] and no one else. /.../ I do not work for someone I don't like.' So when the minister left, the advisor left the government offices to work for an interest organization.

Others are more loyal to specific organizations, as this political advisor of a struggling party recounts:

> Then she [the headhunter] came back with a different offer without the disadvantages I had identified earlier, but I still said no. Then I realized that I actually wanted to take this the whole way. That I felt a loyalty and that I didn't want to leave when the polls looked so bad. I did not want to betray them.

Ideological commitment and specific loyalties are important not only to policy professionals but also to the organizations that hire them. No party or other organization would hire someone whose ideological commitment and loyalty could not be trusted, which would often be the case if they had ever worked for ideological opponents (Svallfors 2016: 66). A personnel officer at a Swedish trade union states that it would be 'very strange if you came here from a career in the employer federation, or vice versa' and maintains that there are very few examples of this. As shown, this is corroborated by our data. Conversely, proven loyalty and ideological commitment increase the market value of policy professionals within their ideological camp.

As discussed, many policy professionals cannot envisage a career outside their current field, but some do choose to exit from the field. Some of these exiters clearly articulate fatigue with the demanding world of policy professionalism and with the stressful life it entails. For those who exit from the policy professional field, elected office is rarely the destination. Being a politician is seen as even harder work than being a policy professional, and as less fun. Instead, they opt for public administration or private companies, which offer better pay for less work and less pressure.

Hence, policy professionalism is to a very limited extent a training ground for elected politics. Few move into elected office and few express any willingness to do so. Rather, policy professionals are choosing an alternative political·career, which runs between various non-elected and yet highly political positions.

In summary, despite the broad avenues that open up to policy professionals because of the specific skills they possess, there are (partly self-placed) hurdles, or even barriers, related to skill varieties, ideological commitments, and loyalties. These factors govern the careers of policy professionals. Even though the majority of policy professionals choose to stay within the field, because it offers power, interesting tasks, and relatively good financial compensation, the world of politics is stressful and demanding, including for policy professionals. This is why some of them choose the exit ramp to private companies or public administration.

CONCLUSION: DISSOLVING OF INSTITUTIONAL BOUNDARIES

As made clear in this chapter, there is now a fairly extensive labour market in which political skills are bought and sold. This indicates a more thorough pro-fessionalization of politics than the one related to elected politicians becoming full-time employees rather than part-time laypersons. Policy professionals typically possess large quantities of human and social capital associated with politics and policy making. This in itself contributes to political inequality by enlarging the skill gulf between ordinary citizens and party/organization members on the one hand and the professionalized political stratum on the other.

But since these specific skills have a comparatively small market outside the policy professional field, policy professionals face certain labour market problems. For example, who will hire a recent exiter from the government offices for a reasonably exciting and well-paid job? Policy professionals' skills are hard to evaluate outside their particular labour market niche; they are highly dependent on their local context, which makes transitions to other settings difficult; and they are deeply attached to their specific line of business.

This 'golden cage' problem is alleviated by the rise of a lobbying or communication advice sector, including both specialized firms and growing public affairs divisions in large companies, where the skills of policy pro-fessionals are in demand and where the true market value of their skills can be estimated. Profit-oriented actors have a great incentive to track and affect political decision making. Therefore, they need politically savvy employees, regardless of whether these are hired on a temporary basis through a PR firm or are permanently employed in-house. Hence, the rise of policy professionals also implies a blurring of institutional boundaries between government, civil society organizations, and private business, something we will return to in the concluding chapter.

The chapter has also discussed the barriers related to the professionalization of politics and policy making. It is simply not the case that policy professionals have morphed into a specialized corps that can and will take any job where their skills might be in demand. Their field is permeated with loyalties and commitments that substantially affect their career paths and decisions. In sum, we should perhaps speak of a semi-professionalization of politics since it is circumscribed by factors other than the supply of and demand for specific skills. Hence, some of the democratically dubious implications of their rise are ameliorated by the fact that policy professionals are politically committed and divided, like the individuals and organizations they serve.

An important implication of the findings in the chapter concerns the dispersion of political skills to new arenas and actors. What we are witnessing is the policy professionalization of not only the political world but of adjacent fields as well. Knowledge of the political system and specific political skills become keys to success not only in the policy professional field but in any organization or activity that is affected by political decisions (that is to say, most organizations and activities). When policy professionals move into organizations outside their own field, they bring with them their typical modus operandi. In this process, they spread these to organizations (such as profit-oriented companies or public administration) whose primary *raison d'être* is different from political influence-making. This is yet another way in which the boundary-spanning characteristics of policy professionals contribute to blurring institutional boundaries.

What the chapter has made abundantly clear is something we have encountered also in the previous chapters. Most policy professionals are a particular breed of professionals, more wedded to ideology and loyalties than to purely professional considerations, and far more driven by power in its various aspects than by money. Money can be found anywhere in a professional world, and in some lines of business in far greater quantities than in the policy professional field. But political power can be found in few places except here, and this is where policy professionals prefer to be, where power can be executed, challenged, or simply enjoyed.

Power over money. Senator Underwood's misgivings seem to be mistaken. Most policy professionals actually prefer the old stone building to the McMansion in Sarasota.

NOTES

1. This chapter builds on joint work with Niels Selling, who conducted many of the interviews, did the empirical mapping presented in the chapter, and wrote parts of the text. Parts of the chapter have previously been published as Selling, Niels, and Stefan Svallfors, 'The Lure of Power: Career Paths and Considerations among Policy Professionals in Sweden.' *Politics & Policy* 47 (5) (2019): 984–1012.
2. Selection criteria for organizations and positions are explicated in detail in the Methods Appendix.
3. See the Methods Appendix for details.
4. One could suspect that the specific pattern of moves and exits from the government offices was due to the fact that it was a right-wing outgoing government. However, a comparison with the exit of the Social Democratic government in 2006 reveals almost identical patterns to the ones in Table 5.2 (figures available from author).

5. A *manager* is a person who leads an organization. Typical job titles include managing director, chief of staff, and head of office. Individuals who are developing policy proposals are classified as *policy*. Their typical job titles include policy advisor, research officer, and political director. *Communication* includes those whose primary responsibility is to disseminate information and maintain interpersonal relationships with media and politicians. Examples of this category are press secretaries, information officers, communicators, and public affairs experts.
6. See the Methods Appendix for details about the sample.

REFERENCES

Allern, Sigurd. 2011. 'PR, Politics and Democracy.' *Central European Journal of Communication* 12 (1): 125–39.

Barley, Stephen, and Gideon Kunda. 2004. *Gurus, Hired Guns, and Warm Bodies: Itinerant Experts in a Knowledge Economy*. Princeton, NJ: Princeton University Press.

Blanes i Vidal, Jordi, Mirco Draca, and Christian Fons-Rosen. 2012. 'Revolving Door Lobbyists.' *American Economic Review* 102 (7): 3731–48.

Büttner, Sebastian M., Lucia M. Leopold, Steffen Mau, and Matthias Posvic. 2015. 'Professionalization in EU Policy-Making? The Topology of the Transnational Field of EU affairs.' *European Societies* 17 (4): 569–92.

Garsten, Christina, Bo Rothstein, and Stefan Svallfors. 2015. *Makt utan mandat. De policyprofessionella i svensk politik*. Stockholm: Dialogos.

Georgakakis, Didier, and Jay Rowell. 2013. *The Field of Eurocracy. Mapping EU Actors and Professionals*. Basingstoke: Palgrave Macmillan.

Granovetter, Mark S. 1973. 'The Strength of Weak Ties.' *American Journal of Sociology* 78 (6): 1360–80.

Laurens, Sylvain. 2018. *Lobbyists and Bureaucrats in Brussels. Capitalism's Brokers*. New York: Routledge.

Parker, Glenn R. 2009. *Capitol Investments: The Marketability of Political Skills*. Ann Arbor, MI: University of Michigan Press.

Parker, Glenn R., Suzanne L. Parker, and Matthew S. Dabros. 2012. 'The Labor Market for Politicians: Why Ex-Legislators Gravitate to Lobbying.' *Business & Society* 52 (3): 427–50.

Svallfors, Stefan. 2016. 'Out of the Golden Cage: PR and the Career Opportunities of Policy Professionals.' *Politics & Policy* 44 (1): 56–73.

Tyllström, Anna. 2019. 'More Than a Revolving Door: Corporate Lobbying and the Socialization of Institutional Carriers.' *Organization Studies*, https://doi.org/10.1177/0170840619848014.

6.   Lobbying for profits: the Swedish case

with Anna Tyllström

We do not merely destroy our enemies; we change them.
(George Orwell, *1984*)

In this chapter, we present a case study of policy professionals in action, as they indeed struggle to change their enemies.[1] The case is the Swedish health care sector, and the surprising resilience that privatized for-profit welfare provision has shown in what was previously thought of as a social democratic bastion of public provision. The chapter will show what a particular subcategory of policy professionals – those who work as public affairs specialists in large private welfare service companies and as policy experts among the business associations in the field – actually do when they act as policy professionals on behalf of employing organizations and for a specific cause. The chapter will provide an illustrative example of what it entails to use the skills that characterize policy professionals: framing problems, knowing processes, and accessing information. The empirical case is based primarily on interviews with key policy professionals in the private health care sector in order to decide what types of actions they use in their lobbying efforts.

The case displays some fascinating features. If a social scientific observer in the late 1980s had been presented with a line-up of rich Western countries – say Germany, Sweden, the UK, France, and the US – and asked to guess which of these countries would later experience a rapid expansion of for-profit providers of health care, elderly care, and education, few would probably have opted for Sweden. Dominant perspectives on the development of welfare states would presumably have pointed to the power resources of the organized labour movement (Korpi 1980, 1983, 1989), the supportive feedback effects from a universal welfare state on important constituencies dependent on the welfare state (Pierson 1994, 1996), and the public support for the existing welfare arrangements (Svallfors 1991, 1995, 1996) as factors that made Sweden a least-likely case of welfare state privatization.

And yet, three decades later, Sweden has in fact experienced an astonishingly fast growth of for-profit providers of care and services. Although the financing of care and education is still predominantly based on taxation, the actual delivery of such services has to an increasing extent come from for-profit providers. So far, no efforts to scale back the activities of for-profit welfare enterprises have been successful. This is in spite of the fact that public support for such providers remains low and that increasing political conflicts have been registered, not least as a result of failing school results, unanticipated consequences of privatization of welfare services, and public scandals involving private enterprises in the welfare sector (Molander 2017).

Understanding why private welfare companies have managed to become stable actors even when faced with an unfavourable public opinion and a considerable political challenge can be explained only by taking the instrumental activities of policy professionals fully into account. Exercising power as a policy professional includes providing new policy ideas, persuading policy makers of the merits of ideas and proposals, and defending existing beneficial practices and regulations. Hired lobbyists and other policy professionals are important providers of such knowledge, information, and advice, which includes knowledge about both political processes and substantive expertise, as discussed in previous chapters.

This chapter focuses on the conflictual and contested for-profit welfare delivery, and the aim is to show how actions by policy professionals have helped privatization to be so resilient in the face of substantial political conflict and opposition. 'Resilient' simply means that for-profit welfare companies and their business associations have been able to stave off any attempts to impose limitations on profit-taking or any other regulation of the standard operating practices of capitalist firms. The question that is raised in this chapter concerns exactly *how* this has been achieved, and what the specific role of policy professionals in the privatized sector is: what do lobbyists in the for-profit welfare sector actually do in order to pursue their interests?

THE PRIVATIZATION OF THE SWEDISH WELFARE STATE

Health care in Sweden is financed by the regional county councils, while child care, elderly care, and education are administered by the municipalities. In primary care, 42 per cent of clinics are now privately owned, and in the Stockholm capital region, that figure is 65 per cent. The lion's share of private providers are for-profit: 97 per cent of county councils' and 83 per cent of municipalities' expenditure on private welfare is spent on for-profit corporations (SKL 2016). Figure 6.1 shows that the increase in overall staffing in the welfare sector largely comes in the for-profit part of the sector. Here, the number of employees increased by 65 per cent between 2000 and 2015, as compared to a 20 per cent increase in the sector as a whole. Figure 6.2 summarizes the development of expenditures on privately produced welfare in the three largest welfare areas: education, elderly care, and health care over the period 2003–17. As shown, spending has increased considerably over the last decade, and almost all of the increase comes from for-profit providers.

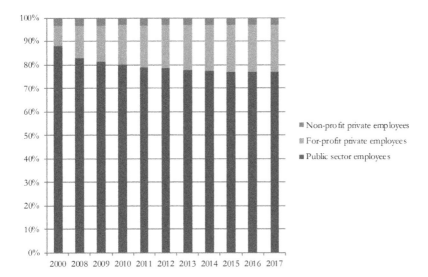

Figure 6.1   *Employees in the Swedish welfare sector 2000–17 according to type of employer, % of total*

Profit-seeking actors in the welfare sector are a fairly new phenomenon in Sweden. Through a series of reforms from the 1940s to the 1960s, welfare policy delivery was centralized and nationalized in the building of the social democratic welfare state. As a result, by the early 1980s, an absolute majority of welfare facilities in Sweden were owned, financed, and run by the public sector. For example, in 1980 only 0.5 per cent of Swedish pupils went to a non-government school.

But this was about to change. Already in the 1980s, local politicians in Nacka, a municipality with a conservative majority, started to experiment with a semi-private arrangement, where the municipality issued vouchers for medical footcare to elderly citizens who could then choose to spend them on private providers (Kastberg 2005). Another important early event was the establishment of the first chain of privately owned preschools, *Pysslingen*, which stirred political debate and ultimately led to *Lex Pysslingen*, a law enforced by the social democratic government to stop all public funding of for-profit preschools.

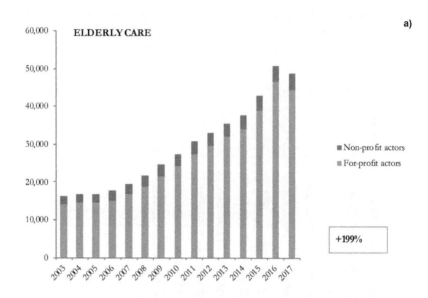

*Figure 6.2   Public expenditure on private health care providers in (a)
            elderly care, (b) education, and (c) health care, 2003–17*

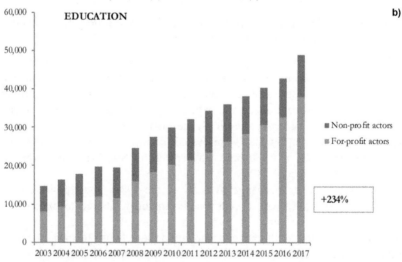

When a coalition of four right-of-centre parties won the national election in
1991, the new government initiated a series of reforms that were intended to
create more choice for citizens and to increase innovation and private entrepreneurship. *Lex Pysslingen* was abolished, and a voucher system, similar

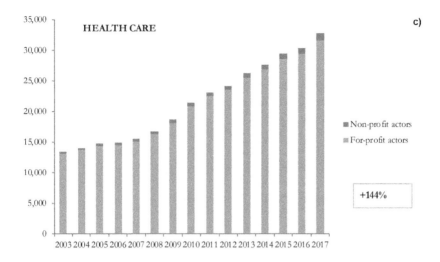

to the footcare voucher, was introduced nationally in the education system. In primary health care, a Family Doctor Reform (*Husläkarreformen*) was introduced in 1993, stipulating that county councils had to apply the same remuneration system to private and public health care providers. This was the starting point for private primary care on a larger scale and was not significantly reversed by later governments (Anell 2011).

Early private actors often operated on contract with county councils or municipalities according to a 'procurer-producer' model, but in later years the system moved more towards a 'consumer's choice' model (Gingrich 2011). Two especially important reforms were the introduction of the Law of Public Procurement (LOU) in 2007, where the guidelines for public sector purchases were formalized, and the (somewhat paradoxically titled) Law of Free Choice System (LOV) in 2009. The latter stipulated that all care facilities fulfilling a series of criteria should be granted the right to public funding if the consumer/patient chooses the services they provide. Municipalities can choose whether to introduce LOV or not; so far, half of the municipalities have done so. County councils are obliged to introduce free choice for primary care, but it is optional for specialized care.

The LOV reform has favoured large corporate groups that benefit from economies of scale. Whereas early private actors often were cooperatives of parents or staff starting their own clinics and centres, in the 2000s national and international corporate groups began to show interest in welfare service provision. As a result, there has been a consolidation of the private care industry. Within education, the ten largest for-profit actors represent 20 per cent of primary education production, and a third of all secondary education

(Skolverket 2014). Within health care, the ten largest firms represent 28 per cent of the turnover among private providers (our own computations based on annual reports).

The privatization of the welfare state has raised considerable controversy. In fall 2011, the 'Carema scandal' exploded in the media. It started with an e-mail to the local government offices containing information from the medically responsible GP at an elderly home run by Carema Care, a for-profit corporate group, stating that she could no longer guarantee the quality of care. When journalists discovered the e-mail, they started scrutinizing the company. They reported on several cases of medical neglect and severe cost reduction programmes. Carema was indirectly owned by overseas venture capitalists with intricate tax planning schemes and generous bonus programmes for managers (see e.g., Lucas and Tottmar 2011). An award-winning documentary was produced by the Swedish Broadcasting Corporation, and more than 4000 media articles were published in two months. The scandal had tangible consequences: several municipalities and county councils cancelled their contracts with the company, which subsequently changed its name. The chief of policy at the private care business association Almega Vårdföretagarna even published a book espousing his perspective on the scandal (Tenelius and Selling 2016). The scandal sparked a wide-ranging political debate about the ethics of profit in the health care sector.

Already in the 2010 election campaign, the fact that venture-capitalist-owned corporations were making profits from tax-financed welfare had started to attract political attention. The Carema scandal brought the issue to the top of the agenda. In later years, criticism has been spurred by more scandals within child care and educational sectors, where privately owned preschools and schools have been accused of putting profit before the quality of education.

Public opinion is clearly against profits in the welfare sector. In Figure 6.3, we can see the development of public opinion. In 2018, 60 per cent of respondents considered prohibition of dividends for publicly financed welfare to be a 'good' or 'very good' idea. Only 19 per cent were against it. In another poll with a slightly different phrasing of the question, in November 2016, 80 per cent preferred a limitation on dividends, and 27 per cent wanted an outright ban (SVT 2016).

There is a clear lack of political representation in the matter. Having championed many of the privatization reforms during their 2006–14 reign, all conservative parties are openly positive to unregulated profits, even though a majority of their voters are negative, resulting in a large discrepancy between party positions and their voters' opinions. This discrepancy is especially tangible in the case of the nativist Sweden Democrats, whose official policy was quite negative to unregulated profits until a very public turnaround in the parliament in 2015. Their voters, however, are approximately as critical as the average: 78 per cent are pro-limitation, and 26 per cent want a ban (SVT 2016).

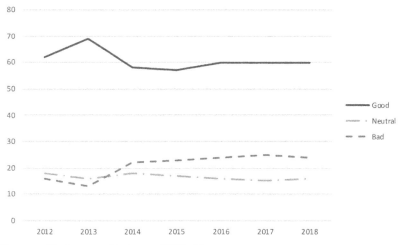

Source: Martinsson and Andersson (2019: 47).

Figure 6.3   *Public opinion attitudes towards the statement 'Profit dividends should not be allowed within tax-financed health care, education, or care', 2012–18*

In early 2015 the government gave directives for a public commission with the task of developing a new framework for regulating the financing of private actors in the public welfare system, the so-called 'Reepalu Commission' (named after its chairperson, a social democratic politician). As is customary, a team of experts and a reference group with representatives from organized interests were attached to the commission. The private welfare sector, headed by the service providers' business association Almega, was from the beginning very strongly opposed to the commission's directives and process. They argued that a cap on profits would severely damage the industry and the welfare sector as a whole. Over the course of the 18 months that the commission worked on its first report, an intricate political interplay took place in the media, public opinion, and the parliamentary committees. The main actors were Almega, the blue-collar trade union LO and its members, and also individual business owners, academics, and investment banks.

In November 2016, the commission's report was released, suggesting a cap of 7 per cent for profits (SOU 2016: 78). In fall 2017, the Social Democratic and Green Party minority government stated their intention to go ahead and propose a law based on the commission, despite the fact that a majority of the parliament was against the proposed law. However, after the election in fall 2018, and following a difficult government formation process, the proposal about a profit cap for private welfare service companies was shelved as part of an agreement settled between the minority government and the Liberal Party and the (market-liberal) Centre Party. The issue of profit caps seems to be politically dead for the foreseeable future, just as the wider issue about the role of profit-making enterprises in the welfare sector is.

To summarize, the Swedish welfare state has been rapidly privatized, although it is still mainly financed by public means. The development has concerned several administrations since the 1980s, and while there have been conflicts between political camps and public opinion has remained largely negative, the main trend has been one of increasing private production of welfare, and then mainly by for-profit actors. Moreover, the development towards for-profit organization of welfare policies has been exceptionally rapid by international standards (Palier 2006).

In the next section, we will take a closer look at the kinds of vigilant activities key actors in the private business community have been engaged in to safeguard the private welfare sector market. It should be emphasized, however, that a focus on these actors does not indicate that other actors (such as political party elites) are of little interest in trying to understand the resilience of for-profit activities. But the lobbyists for the private welfare sector have attracted comparatively little research interest and it is therefore highly motivated to analyse their considered actions and discursive strategies if one wants to understand the resilience of the private welfare sector. Furthermore, in the perspective of this book, the case of defending privatized health services is an interesting case of successful policy professional action in hostile terrain.

POLICY PROFESSIONAL ACTION IN THE PRIVATE WELFARE INDUSTRY

In order to understand what policy professionals actually do in this case, we conducted interviews with three types of policy professionals: business association experts ('BAEs'), public affairs officials or CEOs in private health care companies ('private company officials' or 'PCOs'), and commissioned experts ('CEs'). The seven interviews were conducted in 2016 and followed a semi-structured format. The BAEs and PCOs were chosen because they were prominent in the debate and represented large companies with high stakes in the debate surrounding the policy process. The interview questions mainly concerned the interviewees' political activities around the issue of profits in the health care sector, how they structured their overall political work, what methods they used, which actors they approached, and what arguments they brought forth and why. The CEs were chosen based on their centrality in the debate and the ongoing state commission, and questions to them specifically concerned their interactions with corporations.

The analysis revealed no fewer than nine distinct types of discursive strategies (presented below), which can be grouped into three main types of active organizing efforts: *influencing perceptions*, *organizing actors*, and *facilitating communication*. The first type of action consists of attempts to actively shape other actors' perceptions and understandings. The second type concerns the organization of relationships among actors in the field in order to build alliances. The last type of action aims at affecting how communication with policy makers and the wider public is set up. In the following, we discuss and illustrate each in turn.

Influencing Perceptions

This theme consists of three types of specific actions: (1) creating facts on the ground, (2) producing quality standards, and (3) enacting transparency.

When it comes to influencing perceptions, perhaps the most fundamental action of private welfare companies is that they *create facts on the ground*. The very first attempts to create privately delivered welfare – the footcare vouchers in Nacka – were ingenious in this regard. While it would have been almost impossible to argue against this on principle grounds, it set an example for later privatizations: why should consumer choice in the sector be restricted to footcare and not include, for example, choosing whom to entrust with the care or education of one's children?

Facts on the ground are even more important once large-scale private welfare delivery is in place. The problem for policy makers intent on rolling back privatization is that any attempts to do so risk creating disruption of essential services and hence dissatisfaction among citizens/voters. This is clearly recognized by policy professionals:

> This company where I work now, and others, may say, 'If you change the compensation system in this way, then we cannot work with this, because we cannot handle it' and that is a type of … I wouldn't call it lobbying really, but it is a kind of information. (PCO1)

Or they may make clear to policy makers that they will have a huge problem on their hands if they attempt to limit profitability in the sector: 'If you make this change, that will in the worst case make a lot of companies go bankrupt, and then you have a giant problem to make your elderly care work.' (BAE1)

But companies are also involved in continuously creating new facts on the ground through expanding their market presence. The targets are strategically chosen:

> We have selected about 40 municipalities where we want to be present over time, /.../ based on a few parameters: one, that it is a municipality that will face a big demographic challenge. Where you can see that in this municipality there will be such an increase in the number of elderly people, we look at their current plans and see 'Oh my God, they have no new facilities on the way,' and we can see that this is not going to work. /.../ The second dimension is: 'Is this a municipality that is open to private care?', that is, have they worked with private providers in the past? /.../ And then we try to make contact with them to ask: 'Are you interested in a conversation?' (PCO4)

By strategically using their current position and possibilities for exit as a bargaining threat, and by extending market presence, private welfare companies and their policy professionals try to beat off threats against the privatized market.

The policy professionals in the private welfare industry do additional things to influence perceptions at the interface between private welfare companies and policy makers and the wider public. One of them is *producing quality standards*. This is important for several reasons: it is an attempt to increase trust in and legitimacy for for-profit providers, but it is also important for creating a 'level playing field' for welfare providers and providing long-term planning horizons. They feel confident that they can hold their own compared to the public sector once standards for comparisons have been set, but they worry that comparisons may be biased:

> We like to be clear with how things work at our end, but we would like the county council to be as clear – not least because we have this voucher system that is relevant. /.../ They can make a loss, to put it bluntly, because that is hidden in the whole county council hole ... in that black hole there. (PCO3)

So, in order to increase trust and enact fair comparisons, policy professionals in the welfare industry work systematically with things such as 'ethical platforms', 'quality measures', 'codes of conduct', and other attempts to systematically produce rules and standards for the industry as a whole. It is far better to self-regulate than to have standards externally imposed:

> There are a number of commissions everywhere that have been given a mandate and it's incredibly important that they don't misunderstand how the industry works. So, we work quite a lot with participating in Reepalu's commission, taking part in procurement, quality, standards, and so on. (BAE2)

The production of standards also serves to shift focus from profits to quality. BAEs emphasized how advanced and forthcoming they were in developing their own quality measures, and how they had established quality measurement practices as a requirement for business association membership. They argued that the lack of discussion about quality has been detrimental to the whole debate about privately produced welfare:

> We need good quality measurements, good quality comparisons so that you can see every ... You should be able to see what the users think in every single elderly care home, publicly as well as privately owned. So that you can compare. These are questions we have been championing for a long time, and then you can say that if we had had those things in place in Sweden, quality comparison systems, then this debate wouldn't have turned out this way. Then, the politicians would have felt more confident saying, 'Well, the quality is good in the privately owned care and health care, we can see that in our measurements.' (BAE1)

The emphasis on quality was also clear when instructing member firms in their communication with politicians and media: BAE1 reports telling his members, 'Remember to say that we want national quality indices!' Tellingly, this attempt to shift focus from profits to quality was prominent in the additional directives that were added to the Reepalu Commission in late 2015, after lobbying efforts by the business organizations.

Producing standards is closely connected to the wider issue of how to *enact transparency*: to decide what to show, for whom, at what time. This serves to increase legitimacy by providing partial transparency: 'What is it that they feel insecure about? /.../ What is it that is not transparent enough?' (PCO1)

> Of course there is an extra responsibility for companies that are fully or partly financed from tax money. Of course that requires oversight. Of course that requires transparency. Of course it requires certain rules that you have to bow down to. (PCO2)

But transparency in this general sense is not enough. It is also important to provide policy makers with examples of well-functioning private firms in action:

> This politician should be able to bring with them: 'I was at this home for the elderly and I saw this and that and how it worked' – politicians have a need to somehow relate to reality. (BAE1)

And a commissioned expert concurs:

> [This company] asked us if we wanted to come. Then we've had, it was almost the first thing we got from [the business association representative]: 'Do you want to

visit specific companies? Let me know and I'll arrange for you to see them.' So, we had a standing invitation in that sense, to meet specific companies. (CE2)

At the same time, transparency always remains partial. The inner workings of private welfare firms are bound by company law to remain business secrets, and due to their technical nature, they are also very hard for lay people to understand. For example, one commissioned expert, in talking about the different profit calculation models that are at issue in the debate, states that 'We are probably talking about fewer than 15 persons in the whole of Sweden who can understand these issues' (CE1). Here, private welfare companies have an enormous advantage compared to their opponents in that they employ professionals who understand issues concerning accounting practices, different concepts of profit, and tax schemes, and what they imply for their companies.

Organizing Actors

In the second action type, organizing actors, three sub-strategies are found in our material: (4) mobilizing one's own, (5) persuading the indifferent, and (6) seeking out friends.

The first task is to *mobilize one's own*, which is a much harder task than might be thought. It could easily be imagined that the sector has such a strong common interest in safeguarding conditions for market presence and profitability that little effort would be needed to keep a unified front. This is, however, not the case. The private welfare industry harbours quite substantial heterogeneity among firms: many are quite small, others very large; firms with large outside owners have higher demands for profitability than self-owned companies. Furthermore, they are all competitors: if one firm fails, others will perhaps be able to increase their share of the market. So, it is a constant struggle for policy professionals to keep their own unified when the industry is under threat:

> When the Carema battle began and they read about it in the newspapers, other firms thought that this would affect only a single company: 'We who are so good, this will not affect us.' /.../ When this whole debate about profits got going I think it was exactly so that these small companies, and those companies that were not owned by venture capitalists /.../ they thought that 'well, what if we got rid of these big companies, maybe that would be great.' (BAE1)

Intra-industry interests clash most clearly regarding the importance of profits in welfare, where individual private welfare companies are less persuaded by the importance of pursuing this topic in the debate:

> We have not really entered it. We think it is a pseudo-issue. /.../ We do not demand the right to make profits, we demand the right to make good health care. /.../ Who has an interest in us standing on the barricades and shouting for the right to make profits? (PCO2)

Positions such as these are known to the BAEs and elicit sour remarks:

> [This company] has a view that they stand above [the business association], and [their representative] has felt that 'I have a sort of direct link in, I can solve this myself. I can solve this, there are no problems' /.../ If you sit on the board of [the business association] and make decisions about strategy and have been willing to increase membership fees last year in order to put more emphasis on opinion-forming, then it is a little strange to say in the next moment that 'I do not think this is important.' (BAE2)

So, policy professionals in the business association must strive incessantly to get all member companies to perceive this as a collective struggle, in a way not at all dissimilar to the ones union representatives have to wage in order to keep members in line. Although policy professionals in the business association ultimately work at a mission task provided by their member companies, it often looks more like the agent driving the principal.

But it is not only important to mobilize one's own; it is also important to *persuade the indifferent*: to get parties and organizations on board who have little concern about these specific issues but may hold pivotal power. In this regard, the most important single thing has been the successful attempts of policy professionals in the private welfare industry to persuade the nativist exclusionary Sweden Democrats to make a complete turnaround on the issue, from critics of for-profit welfare to supporters. Because of this, there is now a clear parliamentary majority against regulating profits in the sector. In August 2014, the Sweden Democrats' party leader Jimmy Åkesson had clearly stated that his party wanted to restrict profits in the welfare sector,[2] but only two years later the rhetoric was largely the same as that put forth by the organized business interests. He and economic spokesman Oscar Sjöstedt then published an opinion piece in a business daily arguing that profits were 'pre-conditions and incentives to improve quality and accessibility' in the welfare sector, while a cap was to equate with 'abuse' of the market model. If the state focused on regulating quality standards instead of profits, a natural cap on the profits firms could make would emerge, they argued.[3]

Here, the groundwork of policy professionals was important:

> I have had two meetings with the Sweden Democrats /.../. Both to learn how they see these issues and to explain how we think one should solve this. /.../ The first meeting we had just because we saw that ... well, the Sweden Democrats were pivotal in our issues, so we needed to know what they thought, and they themselves thought 'we know nothing about these issues.' (BAE1)

But attempts to persuade the indifferent are not, of course, limited to the Sweden Democrats: they extend to any party or organization that has an influence on important decisions, but no firm standpoints when it comes to the issue of privatized welfare. When such attempts are successful they are most likely grounded in the strategic interests of the indifferent party – in the case of the Sweden Democrats, their interest in future collaboration with the conservative parties in parliament.

Closely related to persuading the indifferent is trying to *seek out friends* among the opponents. This is helped by the fact that both the Social Democratic Party and unions have been divided on the issues. There are several leading Social Democrats who are quite supportive of for-profit activities in the welfare sector, in spite of the fact that both grassroots members and public opinion are strongly negative.[4] Furthermore, the unions were for a time quite divided: the large public sector union *Kommunal* was in the 1990s and early 2000s quite favourable to privatization because they imagined competing employers in care and education would entail better working conditions and wage prospects (Waldemarson 2010: 379–81). The blue-collar union confederation LO and its member organizations are by now clearly against for-profit welfare delivery. But they are still much less present and active in the influence work and debate than their antagonists are. This is partly a resource issue, where weakened working-class trade unions cannot muster the same level of resources as the richly endowed private welfare sector. Partly it is a question of the relative policy influence of different trade unions, where shifting power relations between blue- and white-collar unions have made the white-collar unions' voice gradually stronger over time (Svallfors 2016). And the white-collar unions take a much more divided stance towards for-profit welfare than the blue-collar unions do. The rifts among the adversaries is clearly recognized and strategically used by policy professionals:

> It is vitally important to meet Social Democrats in important municipalities so we understand: How do they think? Are they pragmatic or are they ideologically far to the left and can they then pose problems?' (BAE1)

In this search for friends among the opponents, they perceive that they score victories: 'We follow the debate every day closely and we note that *no* leading

Social Democrat enters the debate on profits any longer. No Green Party activist, that was a long time ago we saw anything of that sort.' (BAE1)

Even when no clear victories can be registered, it is still very important to keep up contacts 'behind enemy lines' so as to be able to activate such neutral or friendly actors in the opposing camp.

Facilitating Communication

The last activity type, facilitating communication, is conducted in three ways: (7) representing public sentiments, (8) opening and closing channels, and (9) customizing messages to policy makers.

First, it is important to *represent public sentiments*. This is important not least because public opinion has been unfavourable towards the opportunities to make profits in the welfare sector, something which the policy professionals in the private welfare sector are now quite aware of:

> You could see that there was … not a majority but there was a very large group of people who were very sceptical about precisely whether you should make a profit and give out dividends. I thought that this was very worrying when I came in here, but when I raised this with our board they said, 'Oh this, it has always looked like this; that is nothing to worry about.' (BAE1)

In this situation, much emphasis has been put on turning public opinion, or at least presenting it in a different light. Such attempts play on the fact that although public opinion concerning profits is quite unfavourable, freedom of choice is quite popular:

> If you ask, 'Is it reasonable that companies can make a profit in the care sector?' then that figure is 40% and very few make the connection that if companies can't make profits, then they can't survive. If they don't survive then there is no possibility to have freedom of choice. (BAE2)

The main and final target for these attempts is not really the public, but rather policy makers:

> We can make the public really feel it is actually not such a great idea to walk in and limit the opportunities for these companies since they actually contribute. Then we want the politicians to feel that maybe I do not have the support to install these regulations, or maybe I should stand up for freedom of choice. Many politicians from the Alliance pushed hard on these issues a decade ago, but now they don't really stand up and they need to feel that they have some wind at their backs and that the public actually likes the alternatives too. (BAE1)

Closely related to opinion building/representation is the need to *open and close channels* of communication with other actors. Policy professionals continually organize meeting grounds for exchange and debate. Not only supporters but also opponents are engaged and challenged in public seminars:

> When we organize seminars about some political issue, we really want both someone who is for and someone who is against. That is important to get an animated debate. (BAE1)

The important thing is not to 'win' every single argument and debate but to keep certain perspectives and issues alive. At the same time, other channels of communication are seen as detrimental to the industry's interest and as something to avoid or close down. For example, one PCO states, 'I don't want my owners to talk about health care' (PCO4) since the owners know little about health care activities and facilities, and bringing them into the debate would risk leading to a focus on profits and tax schemes that would be unfortunate for the cause. But most of all it was the Reepalu Commission that was the object of the policy professionals' ire:

> What is troublesome is that this commission still sits. Because we think that the debate has changed /.../
> *So you want to close down this commission?*
> Yes! [laughs] Or that it gets new directives – that would be great. (BAE1)
> I would like to put the lights out for this commission, absolutely. (BAE2)

By opening and closing channels, policy professionals try to make sure that the debate is pursued on terms which are beneficial for their cause, and by suitable actors. Theirs is not an academic interest in debate for argument's sake but debate to further and consolidate interests.

The last, but not least, way in which policy professionals in the private welfare sector act to further their companies' interests is by *customizing messages for policy makers*. This has several aspects. One is the importance of good timing – approaching politicians and other policy makers at a time when issues are on the table, not too early and not too late. Here, political experience is the basis for sound advice:

> Now is not a good time to seek out politicians to talk about this – why should you do that? They are not into that now, the yearly cycle in politics is a given a long time beforehand. They do not get into budget work and think about what they will put their money on until ... or if they should procure something, they don't do that until next fall! (PCO1)

In this regard, it is of fundamental importance to have first-hand political experience: you have to know the nooks and crannies of political decision making
and how political logic differs from business logic:

> There are many of us in this company who know politics. /.../ Everybody does not
> have to have [political experience], but we who reason and make decisions about
> how to make contact with politicians, that is, when we do it, how we do it, and how
> we pursue that dialogue. /.../ Political logic and business logic, they are two com-
> pletely different worlds and often they do not meet. (PCO3)

So, in accessing policy makers, it is key not only to have the right timing but
to frame arguments in a way that will land well in political quarters, and here
previous experience is invaluable:

> It has to do with both tonality and about understanding the rationality of politics.
> If you want to achieve change you have to understand a bit about 'what's in it for
> me?' Because if I come and you're the politician, and I just state that 'I think you
> are doing the wrong thing. Do this instead!' then it is very rarely possible to have
> a dialogue, but [instead it's better] if you come to the politician and say, 'I can see
> that you have a problem; this could be a way to solve it.' (PCO3)

Hence, customizing messages for policy makers in an optimal way requires
considerable political know-how, skills that can only be acquired by first-hand
experience, which is why so many companies and organizations hire people
with such experience (cf. Chapter 5).

In Table 6.1 we summarize in stylized form the particular policy professional skills that are important for each of the action types we have discerned.
As shown, all three skills are to some extent necessary for each of the action
types, but for each action type some skills are more important than others.
The skill of knowing the game and of framing problems is on average more
important than accessing information, perhaps as an effect of the fact that
privatization lobbying is not so dependent on information about and from the
government offices. Being able to frame problems in the right way is very
important for most action types, as is the ability to know whom to approach
among decision makers and how to approach them.

To sum up, safeguarding the market for private welfare companies is
a relentless pursuit, which has to be conducted using a broad array of strategic
discursive actions and applying a broad set of political skills. Hence, the particular acquired skills of policy professionals become essential in the process,
something to which we will return in the concluding section of the chapter.

Table 6.1   Action types and policy professional skills

	Framing problems	Knowing the game	Accessing information
Create facts on the ground	X	x	*X*
Produce quality standards	*X*	x	X
Enact transparency	*X*	X	x
Mobilize one's own	X	X	(x)
Persuade the indifferent	X	X	(x)
Seek out friends	X	X	(x)
Represent public sentiments	*X*	X	x
Open and close channels	x	*X*	x
Customize messages to policy makers	X	*X*	x

Note: *X* = Very important; X = Quite important; x = Somewhat important; (x) = Not so important.

CONCLUSION: DEFENDING PRIVATIZATION THROUGH POLICY PROFESSIONALISM

In this chapter, we have charted the development of for-profit welfare delivery in Sweden, from the first fledgling attempts in the early 1980s until today, when an extensive part of welfare policies are delivered by for-profit companies. In order to understand why this industrial-welfare complex has been so resilient against political backlash we need to take seriously action by private companies and their organizations, as they try to guarantee continuous access to the vast resource pool that is the welfare state.

In short, we need to analyse not only how organized actors try to influence other parties' actions directly, but also their attempts to shape how they *think*. Consequently, the bulk of the empirical analysis in the chapter concerns the discursive strategic action in the private welfare sector, and we discern a number of ways in which private health care companies and their organizations act to influence perceptions, organize actors, and facilitate communication: they create facts on the ground, produce quality standards, enact transparency, mobilize, persuade, seek out friends, represent public sentiments, open and close channels, and customize messages to policy makers.

One perhaps particularly noteworthy aspect of the analysis is what it reveals about the relation between the welfare companies and policy professionals in their main business association. What the analysis shows is that specific policy professionals lodged in this association seem to be the driving part in the relation. Rather than simply working on a mission provided by the members, the policy professionals in the business association take on themselves the role of advanced policy/political guides and act as ideological persuaders and enforcers versus the member enterprises. The agent often seems to be driving the principal, rather than the other way around. That policy professionals often are far more than simple executers and deliverers for their employing organizations transpires here in almost stylized form.

By providing an illustration from a specific case, the chapter has pointed to what policy professionalism may consist of in everyday practice. Knowledge about the political system and its specific logics and actors, the ability to frame problems in certain ways and not others, and the access to crucial information are all necessary ingredients to become and stay a successful policy actor regarding the future of the welfare state. Hence, the discursive strategies of policy professionals in this specific field and subcategory illustrate what acting as a policy professional may entail.

What we have therefore shown in this chapter is the broad array of activities that policy professionals lodged in private welfare companies and their associations pursue, activities that have so far been quite successful in staving off challenges to the for-profit sector in welfare policy delivery. We suggest that such activities should be attended to if one wants to understand how resilient privatization has proved to be in what was previously thought of as extremely hostile territory for such ventures. They contribute to the 'lock-in' of a large sector of for-profit facilities financed by the public purse. Whereas 'lock-in' used to underpin a collectively financed and publicly organized welfare state (Pierson 1994, 1996), in the new privatized environment it works to make a roll-back of for-profit facilities very hard to achieve. Practical 'facts on the ground' now make risk-averse politicians hesitant about risking a head-on collision with the for-profit companies and their associations. The whole issue about restricting profit-making activities in the welfare sector seems to be dead and buried, in a country that used to brandish the social democratic hegemony par excellence. Perhaps Swedish welfare lobbyists do not destroy their enemies, but they certainly change them.

NOTES

1. This chapter builds on joint work with Anna Tyllström, who conducted all the interviews, did the empirical analysis behind Figures 6.1–6.3, and wrote parts of the text. Parts of the chapter have previously been published as Svallfors, Stefan, and Anna Tyllström, 'Resilient Privatization: The Puzzling Case of For-Profit Welfare Providers in Sweden.' *Socio-Economic Review* 17 (3) (2019): 745–65.
2. 'Jimmie Åkesson frågas ut inför valet', SR 140828, http://sverigesradio.se/sida/avsnitt/423608?programid=4657 (accessed 1 December 2017).
3. Jimmie Åkesson and Oscar Sjöstedt, Vinsttaket är ett övergrepp, *Dagens Industri*, 160909, https://www.di.se/artiklar/2016/9/9/debatt-vinsttaket-ar-ett-overgrepp/ (accessed 1 December 2017).
4. Some examples are Lars Stjernkvist, chair of the municipality board of one of the larger cities in Sweden, Norrköping: http://www.svt.se/opinion/det-ar-fel -att-forbjuda-valfardsforetag-som-fungerar-bra; the leading Stockholm politician Karin Wanngård: http://www.di.se/nyheter/s-revolt-mot-reepalus-vinsttak/; and the newspaper editor Widar Andersson: http://www.dagenssamhalle.se/kronika/ vagar-reepalu-ta-miljardaerens-parti-14181 (websites accessed 1 December 2017).

REFERENCES

Anell, Anders. 2011. 'Hälso-och sjukvårdstjänster i privat regi.' In *Konkurrensens konsekvenser. Vad händer med svensk välfärd?*, edited by Laura Hartman, pp. 181–214. Stockholm: SNS.

Gingrich, Jane. 2011. *Making Markets in the Welfare State. The Politics of Varying Market Reforms.* New York: Cambridge University Press.

Kastberg, Gustaf. 2005. *Kundvalsmodeller. En studie av marknadsskapare och skapade marknader i kommuner och landsting.* Göteborg: Göteborg University.

Korpi, Walter. 1980. 'Social Policy and Distributional Conflict in the Capitalist Democracies: A Preliminary Comparative Framework.' *West European Politics* 3 (3): 296–316.

Korpi, Walter. 1983. *The Democratic Class Struggle.* London: Routledge and Kegan Paul.

Korpi, Walter. 1989. 'Power, Politics, and State Autonomy in the Development of Social Citizenship: Social Rights during Sickness in Eighteen OECD Countries since 1930.' *American Sociological Review* 54 (3): 309–28.

Lucas, Dan, and Mia Tottmar. 2011. 'Caremas ökande vinster hamnar i skatteparadis.' *DN*, 2011-11-09, http://www.dn.se/sthlm/caremas-okande-vinster-hamnar-i -skatteparadis/ (accessed 1 December 2017).

Martinsson, Johan, and Ulrika Andersson. 2019. *Svenska trender 1986–2018.* Göteborg: SOM-Institutet Göteborgs universitet.

Molander, Per. 2017. *Dags för omprövning – en ESO-rapport om styrning av offentlig verksamhet.* Stockholm: Rapport till Expertgruppen för studier i offentlig ekonomi.

Palier, Bruno. 2006. *Hälso-och sjukvårdens reformer: En internationell jämförelse.* Stockholm: SKL.

Pierson, Paul. 1994. *Dismantling the Welfare State? Reagan, Thatcher, and the Politics of Retrenchment.* Cambridge: Cambridge University Press.

Pierson, Paul. 1996. 'The New Politics of the Welfare State.' *World Politics* 48 (2): 143–79.

SKL. 2016. Köp av verksamhet 2015. Kommuner, landsting och regioner 2006–2015. Stockholm: Sveriges Kommuner och Landsting.

Skolverket. 2014. Privata aktörer inom skola och förskola.

SOU. 2016:78. Ordning och reda i välfärden – betänkande i välfärdsutredningen. Stockholm.

Svallfors, Stefan. 1991. 'The Politics of Welfare Policy in Sweden: Structural Determinants and Attitudinal Cleavages.' *British Journal of Sociology* 42: 609–34.

Svallfors, Stefan. 1995. 'The End of Class Politics? Structural Cleavages and Attitudes to Swedish Welfare Policies.' *Acta Sociologica* 38: 53–74.

Svallfors, Stefan. 1996. *Välfärdsstatens moraliska ekonomi: välfärdsopinionen i 90-talets Sverige*. Umeå: Boréa.

Svallfors, Stefan. 2016. 'Politics as Organized Combat – New Players and New Rules of the Game in Sweden.' *New Political Economy* 21 (6): 505–19.

SVT. 2016. Majoritet vill begränsa vinster i välfärden.

Tenelius, Håkan, and Niels Selling. 2016. *Välfärdslobbyisten. Om Caremadrevet, vårdvinster och demokratins nya utmaningar*. Stockholm: Ekerlids.

Waldemarson, Ylva. 2010. *Mellan individ och kollektiv: Kommunal 1960–2010*. Stockholm: Premiss.

7. Policy professionals and the future of democracy

The year is 1951. The young senator Lyndon B. Johnson has persuaded Senate majority leader Richard Russell to accept help and support from one of Johnson's staffers. Russell is hesitant at first; he is used to doing all the important work himself and does not think any staffer could possibly be up to the task. But, as told by historian Robert Caro, he soon changes his mind:

> Richard Russell had never had an assistant like George Reedy. Sometimes they would be alone together in Russell's office in the evenings, and Russell found himself discussing the strategy for the hearings – not specific questions or press releases but the overall *strategy* – and he found that Reedy was worth discussing strategy with, that it helped to bounce ideas off him, to get other sides of the issue. /.../ By the conclusion of the MacArthur hearings, Russell understood the importance – the *necessity* – of staff, of the way in which it could enable a senator, could enable the *Senate*, to deal with the new complexities, the complexities that had been overwhelming senators and the Senate. He understood the importance of this tool in modern politics.[1]

That was the 1950s, but George Reedy is now everywhere. His ilk is found all around the democratic world – in parliamentary back offices, in political party headquarters, in government offices, in think tanks, in business associations' and trade unions' policy expert functions, and not least among lobbying firms and communication advice bureaus. They no longer include only young white males working for middle-aged white males; they come in various shapes and colours and include as many women as men. But they are all highly skilled in the arts of politics and policy making, they are knowledgeable professionals with large sway, and they have become far more than the simple 'tools' that Senator Russell envisaged.

This has been a book about this particular set of political actors – policy professionals – and their skills, actions, networks, motivations, and careers. The main empirical locus for the book has been Sweden – once the archetypical corporatist social democratic welfare state – but additional perspectives have been added from other comparable European countries.

As argued throughout the book, policy professionalism is a particular form of politics and policy making. This form is different from both the standard elected politics of representation and responsibility, and from public administration as conducted by specialists who are recruited based on merits. Policy professionalism is not a new phenomenon, as illustrated by George Reedy and his generational comrades. But it is a phenomenon that has grown in size, spread, and significance over the course of the last few decades in virtually the whole democratic world.

In this concluding chapter, I intend not only to summarize the most important findings and arguments from the previous chapters, I also want to address three interconnected broader themes related to the actions and skills of policy professionals. The first one deals with the interrelations between the field that policy professionals inhabit, their particular skills, and their motivations. These interrelations result in a special entrepreneurial ethos and orientation towards their chosen field of occupation, with far-ranging ramifications for politics and democracy. The second theme concerns the fraught relationship between democracy and expertise, and the specific angle that policy professionalism brings to this long-standing problem. Policy professionals are first and foremost experts on politics itself, which makes their professionalization and professionalism different from other forms of expertise. The last theme, on which the book closes, is the role of policy professionals for the current state and future development of political power and political inequality in democratic societies. Democracy has (once again) entered troubled waters, and the role of policy professionals in the current situation needs to be properly understood.

Before entering into this extended discussion we need to remind ourselves of the most important arguments and findings in previous chapters. They have delved into three broad and interconnected empirical themes: the skills and resources of policy professionals (Chapter 3), the motivations and attractions of life as a policy professional (Chapter 4), and the careers and career considerations among policy professionals (Chapter 5). In addition, a case study of policy professionals in action was provided, in which the discursive actions of Swedish lobbyists in the private welfare sector were analysed (Chapter 6).

Regarding skills and resources, I highlighted the peculiar 'glocal' nature of policy professionals. Their skills are highly generic across contexts: policy professionals do very similar things and use very similar skills and resources regardless of national context. At the same time, the application of such skills and resources is very much locally dependent on access to relevant networks and information. Moving from one national context to the other would almost mean starting from scratch again, and few policy professionals would consider that.

The skills of policy professionals can be summarized as the ability to frame problems, to know the game, and to access information. Their application includes describing contemporary society from an angle that benefits the values and groups that one represents, and to suggest possible policy solutions.

But it also includes knowing where in the complex political system decisions are really made, who the key actors are in a specific issue, when you have to act in the policy process, and how you should best present your concerns to political decision makers. And it also includes getting fast access to information and correct data, to be used for the causes one wants to pursue.

Networks are of fundamental importance for policy professionals in providing access to relevant information, getting to know who is who in the political landscape, and figuring out how processes are shaped so one can also shape them. And the space for relevant political action is contested, with diffuse and fleeting boundaries and sometimes unclear mandates. A constant renegotiation and appropriation of space becomes as necessary as network building and maintenance. Such negotiations about space and network building differ in importance among various policy professionals, but they are hardly completely absent anywhere. They attest to the boundary-spanning nature of the work of policy professionals.

Regarding the motivations and attractions of life as a policy professional, the key driving force is power, in its different guises. This includes power as agency, to be able to make a difference as a political actor, in things small or big. It also includes power as proximity, to be close to power and in the rooms where important decisions are made, to take part in all the buzz and excitement. And it also includes power as self-determination, to be able to keep control over what one does and says and organize work as one sees fit. The importance of these various aspects of power varies among policy professionals, and there is sometimes a trade-off between them, but policy professionals are typically attracted by all three guises of power.

Most policy professionals have little desire to become elected politicians, but the reasons why they hold this view vary between national contexts. To summarize in stylized fashion: Swedish policy professionals emphasize the slow and boring nature of political careers combined with relentless media pressure; their Latvian counterparts detest the semi-corrupt, uneducated, and unseemly aspects of politics; Irish policy professionals are bothered by the needs for politicians to pander to the petty issues of local constituents – the tyranny of localism; while their Dutch colleagues are bored by the hollow and personalized politics in a consensus-driven polity.

Furthermore, policy professionals typically claim that they are not politicians, a view that is held also among political advisors who work closely with elected and appointed politicians. But a minority actually claim that they are politicians, and even among those who claim they are not politicians, attitudes are fairly ambivalent. They are politicians in the sense that they affect political decisions and processes, but they are not politicians because they are not ultimately responsible for decisions and responsive to voters. And this is exactly what is attractive about being a policy professional.

Policy professionals have very mixed views about elected politicians. Many respect or even admire leading politicians (such as ministers and party leaders); this goes particularly for political advisors who have been personally recruited by 'their' minister or MP. The average politicians get more mixed reviews: most are seen as hard-working, but some are seen as lazy. Not many are seen as particularly bright, but a few are seen as really sharp. All in all, few policy professionals are particularly impressed by the intellectual acumen of the average politician.

Ideological commitment and personal or organizational loyalty are important for most policy professionals. These were factors that helped bring them into their line of business in the first place, and they tend to remain important in their daily work. It goes in particular for those who work for political parties and trade unions, but ideological commitment and value-based enterprise are found even among the most marketized of policy professionals, such as lobbyists and other consultants.

Regarding policy professional careers, it is power rather than money that is the main driving force behind decisions to remain in a position, to move to other policy professional positions, or to exit from the field. An analysis of trajectories of Swedish policy professionals also revealed that there are clear ideological barriers in the field; no one ever moves between political parties or between think tanks, for example, and transitions between trade unions and business associations were extremely rare. There is considerable flux among different positions in the policy professional field, where the specific skills of policy professionals are in demand across a broad segment of employing organizations.

And yet, policy professionals face a 'golden cage' problem in that their true skills and abilities are hard to evaluate for employing organizations outside the policy professional field. Here, the PR and lobbying sector act as 'bridges' to the world of private business. Very few policy professionals ever become full-time politicians, thus acting on their expressed desire to stay out of elected politics, while most also shun public administration since it is considered too uninspiring compared to working in the policy professional field.

The case study of policy professionals in action concerned the Swedish health care sector and the discursive actions of business association experts and public affairs specialists as they have successfully defended profit-making by private companies in the publicly funded health care system. In a relentless pursuit, this special segment of policy professionals has managed to influence perceptions, organize actors, and facilitate communication in their domain. Their action repertoire includes creating facts on the ground to lock in institutional achievements, producing quality standards to pre-empt regulation, enacting transparency to build trust, mobilizing one's own for the cause, persuading the indifferent, seeking out friends in the enemy camp, representing public sentiments to decision makers, opening and closing channels of communication, and customizing suitable messages to policy makers. This action repertoire builds on the various skills of policy professionals in framing problems, knowing the political game and accessing information.

THE ENTREPRENEURIAL ETHOS

The analyses in this book give reason to reflect on a set of broader issues related to political power, democracy, and professionalization. The first relates to the particular ethos and orientation towards their work that policy professionals espouse in their mission. As put in Chapter 4, this could be summarized as an entrepreneurial ethos. Needless to say, 'entrepreneurial' in this sense does not mean coming up with new commodities and finding ways to marketize them. But it is entrepreneurial in the sense of coming up with new political ideas and policy proposals, and finding ways to persuade policy makers and/or the wider public about their merits so that they can be put into action.

This means that *innovation* becomes the ultimate goal for policy professionals. Innovation primarily means to introduce something new, and to be able to present and sell this something new to others. According to economist Joseph Schumpeter, who remains the prime theorist on entrepreneurship, being an innovator is somewhat different from being an inventor. The innovator does not typically discover or create new things as the inventor does, but is able to turn inventions into products (Croitoru 2012: 145). In a similar way, policy professionals are rarely the inventors of particular theories and perspectives, but innovators that can put such theories and perspectives to use in politics and policy making.

Hence, policy professionals use their skills not only to design policy proposals and suggest new perspectives, they also use these skills to get their ideas channelled into the political system and ultimately into laws and policies. They have to be attentive to the opening and closing of windows of opportunity, or even try to open or close such windows themselves. Like other innovators, they have to accept that not all ideas will fly, and they have to swallow that they often cannot take credit for what they achieve. But this is all part of the rules of their game, and the persistent innovator will not be deterred by temporary or even repeated let-downs.

For this entrepreneurial ethos to become fully operational, policy professionals need their particular political skills but also, as explained in Chapter 2, their social skills in being able to get people to work for them and their causes. It means activating their networks in order to get both input for their own thinking and channels for dissemination of ideas and suggestions. Without functioning connections, policy professionals would work in a vacuum and their work would travel nowhere.

Having an entrepreneurial ethos and orientation towards politics and policy making is essentially different both from the politician's and the public administrator's ethos and orientation. In the case of politicians, their ethos should be based in responsibility and responsiveness (Weber 1919 [1977]). They are responsible to citizens and voters for their actions and can (and should) be voted out of office if they fail to meet their expectations. They should be responsive to the wishes of the electorate and try to do what their voters want them to do. They should be regularly exposed to evaluation and judgement, even by people who understand little about politics and policy making. Public administrators should be animated by a sense of the common good and by aspirations to impartiality and integrity. They should serve the public (or the representatives of the public) under the law and be subject to removal from office if they fail in this objective (Lundquist 1998).

Such a description of the differing ethos and orientations of politicians and public administrators could be perceived as utterly naïve. Of course, some or even many politicians dodge responsibility and fail to be responsive to their voters; of course, some public administrators are dishonest, partial, and self-interested; of course, voters are often ignorant and inattentive (Achen and Bartels 2016). But the mere fact that trust is breached and responsibilities avoided is not a case for dismissing these basic orientations and expectations. Transgressions are only perceived as such because there are institutionalized expectations of a particular behaviour in the roles as politician or public administrator.

None of these expectations are present in the case of policy professionals. They are not elected and are not responsible before a public of any kind. They are not public administrators but hired to do politics, in the broad sense of trying to affect policies from a particular perspective based in certain interests and values. They are good entrepreneurs if they manage to transmit new ideas and perspectives and put them into practice, they are bad entrepreneurs if they fail in this. They do not respond to calls of responsiveness from the public or from the civil service code of conduct; they are judged by their employers on the basis of how successfully they can transform or defend existing politics and policies.

If we compare the role and ethos of policy professionals with those of politicians and public administrators we find a particular combination of agency and responsibility. Politicians have a high degree of agency coupled with being ultimately responsible for decisions and actions. Public administrators' degree of agency is much lower (circumscribed by institutional design and by policy makers' decisions) and they are not ultimately responsible for the contents of decisions, only for their correct implementation. Policy professionals are neither this nor that. They are able to combine a fair degree of agency with very little responsibility to a wider public or electorate. In their happiest moments they can therefore maximize freedom, both in the sense of being free to act and create and in the sense of not having to submit to judgement by the ignorant. Hence the attractions of their line of work.

The entrepreneurial ethos may be cast in either a bright or a darker light. The bright side would be that in this dedication to innovation a number of highly competent and skilled people contribute to addressing important social and political problems. They provide inspiration for the ultimate policy makers and increase the repertoire of possible policy solutions. They are both sounding boards and idea incubators for decision makers.

The dark side would be that the entrepreneurial mode of doing politics tends to sideline democratic procedures or turn them on their heads. If new political ideas, arguments, and proposals are formulated by policy professionals, who successfully persuade organizational leadership about their merits and then help to foist them on a largely passive membership, the democratic character of organizations and parties turns into a charade. The scope of this book does not include deciding on which of these scenarios has stronger empirical support, but it seems important to highlight possible consequences of an entrepreneurial ethos in action.

DEMOCRACY AND POLITICAL EXPERTISE

The rise and gradually more accentuated role of policy professionals in politics and policy making provides a new angle to the old question of the relation between democracy and expertise. The particular form of professionalization that they embody raises questions about how this relation unfolds over time and how it should ideally be constructed. This is because policy professionals are primarily experts in politics itself, and in the art of policy advocacy, rather than in any specific subject field.

Democracy and expertise have always had something of a fraught relationship. This could be described as a tension between the notion of popular *sovereignty*, that a people (however defined) should be able and allowed to govern itself in all matters through its elected representatives, and the request that government should be *enlightened* in the sense of relying on truth and the best available evidence for its decisions (Holst and Molander 2019). This tension has been traditionally resolved by a sort of compromise between democracy and expertise so that democracy has become self-limiting in leaving large areas of decision making to professionals and civil servants. Ultimate goals have been decided by elected representatives while professional judgement has been applied about the best means to achieve them. We do not vote on scientific experiments, surgical methods, or how to construct bridges, or even which literature should receive public support; we let experts decide. And politicians do not decide on the day-to-day operations of public authorities; they are run by public administrators applying general directions from government under the rule of law. Such a division of labour between politics and public administration has as an important precondition the separation of political and administrative careers, so that politicians and public administrators have different incentives and act as each other's supervisors (Dahlström and Lapuente 2017).

In the Swedish case, the celebrated 'Swedish model' was always an expert-grounded and expert-driven enterprise. As put by political scientist Sven Steinmo, Swedish policy making tended towards 'governing as an engineering problem', in which the presence and active policy-formation role of experts on, say, taxes, social insurance, and the labour market was prominent indeed (Steinmo 2012).

The compromise between democracy and expertise has lately come under attack from two quite different quarters. One is from a democratic populism, according to which winning elections should allow winners to decide on all matters, including those that were previously considered out of bounds for democratic decision making (Müller 2016: Ch. 2). An almost opposite critique comes from the turn to 'epistocracy', in which it is claimed that all democratic decision making should be guided by truth and knowledge, and that democracy without truth is destructive and self-dissolving (see the discussion in Holst and Molander 2019). Here it is often claimed that democracy needs to be guided by expert bodies not only in matters of technical detail but in formulating the political goals themselves. In its extreme versions, this critique claims that only citizens that pass a certain threshold of knowledge should even be allowed to vote or run for office, and more generally that political power should be distributed according to skill and knowledge (Brennan 2016). Such a turn towards 'epistocracy' has been fuelled by the recent populist surge in democratic societies, which many times has defied established knowledge and descended into a 'war on truth' with disastrous democratic and social consequences (Rothstein 2019).

Regardless of the perils and shortcomings of each of these opposite critiques, the rise of the policy professionals provides a different angle to the question of the relation between democracy and expertise. Policy professionals are not primarily experts in any particular subject field, but in politics and policy advocacy. Even if some of them are indeed experts in some specific policy field, their distinguishing feature lies elsewhere, in knowing the political and policy-making game. They are experts on how to access politically relevant information, how to frame political problems, how to navigate the nooks and crannies of the political decision-making machinery. In this case, the conflict between democracy and expertise takes on a particularly urgent character. What is at stake here is the ability to translate values and interests into effective action, not primarily by being more knowledgeable about the issues themselves but by being more skilled in the processes of politics and policy making. Here, the knowledge gap between citizens/voters/members and policy professionals becomes something of a democratic problem in itself.

This is exactly the democratic problem on which political scientist Robert Dahl closed his magnum opus *Democracy and Its Critics*: 'I am inclined to think that the long-run prospects for democracy are more seriously endangered by inequalities in resources, strategic positions, and bargaining strength that are derived not from wealth or economic position but from special knowledge,' states Dahl (1989: 333), and he claims that these democratic dangers stem from 'the influence of a particular subset of intellectuals who are essential to the intelligent functioning of the modern political systems (democratic or not) – those who are particularly concerned with public policy and actively engaged in influencing government decisions, not only directly but also indirectly through their influence on public and elite opinions' (Dahl 1989: 334). In other words, exactly the 'subset of intellectuals' that this book targets.

Dahl points to increasing political complexity as the prime driver of the increased presence and significance of these political specialists and claims that a 'quasi guardianship' may be the end result, which although it 'might draw the final curtain on the democratic vision', 'would not inaugurate rule by true guardians who possess the wisdom and virtue necessary to political knowledge' (Dahl 1989: 338). Such a dismal development does not, Dahl emphasizes, come about through cunning scheming from the policy elites; their role is more or less thrust upon them. In the terms of this book, most policy professionals harbour a strong attachment to the values and practices of democracy and political equality, and yet their activities could easily serve to undermine these very values and practices.

At the same time, Dahl stresses that there is cause for guarded optimism, based on 'the diversity of views among policy specialists and the relative weakness of their common interests as a "class"' (Dahl 1989: 339). This is something this book has made clear in pointing to how ideological divisions structure the careers and networks of policy professionals. They are not about to morph into a unified corps with strong common interests; they are just as divided as the constituents and leaderships they serve (or sometimes lead). This provides some hope that the democratic implications of the rise of this particular group of experts may not be as detrimental as Dahl feared.

This is linked to the question of what kind of professional group policy professionals actually constitute. As pointed out, in many ways policy professionals do indeed appear as a professional group among others. They have their own ethos, skill sets, standards for success, and reward systems. And similar to many other professional groups, they to some extent even have their own lingo which may be hard for outsiders to understand. As pointed out in the introduction, policy professionals are particularly similar to new 'hybrid' semi-professionals that combine professional and managerial skills, such as 'itinerant experts' (Barley and Kunda 2004), 'connective professionals' (Noordegraaf, van der Steen, and van Twist 2014), and 'wealth managers' (Harrington 2016).

But in certain and key respects they are different from other professional groups. In contrast to other professional groups, their professionalism is of a particular partisan kind. This partisan element, often combined with a certain patronage element since many policy professionals are tied to the fate of particular politicians or organizational leaders, is something that thwarts a development into a 'pure' form of professionalization (including legitimation, established credentials, etc.). Policy professionals are political and not primarily professional creatures regarding both their motivations and their practices and careers. The strong ideological and value-based component of their work and careers also overrides tendencies towards becoming a 'supra-political' stratum based in professional skills in the political field. No one ever moves between different political parties or between different think tanks, and few people shift sides from business associations to trade unions or vice versa, and policy professionals are not about to be transformed to a specialized corps working for any and all purposes where their skills could be used.

In contrast to other semi- or 'hybrid' professionals, policy professionals face a need for constant democratic legitimization. They cannot afford to be seen as working against the values and interests of their constituencies (such as members), regardless of whether these are members of democratic organizations or paying customers. But they also cannot afford to be seen as acting to undermine democracy in any way; even the most clear-cut cases of hired hands, such as lobbyists and communication advisors, claim to be ultimately strengthening democracy through their work. Such demands for democratic legitimation are not there for other semi- or 'hybrid' professions, since these demands stem from the political core of the work of policy professionals.

As has been repeatedly shown in this book, policy professionals sometimes or even often are much more than agents, much more than the 'tools' Richard Russell discovered. We find repeated instances where the agents seem to be driving the principals, either by simply coming up with new useful things that can be applied in different settings or by actually inducing principals to work in a specific direction. Policy professionals are not simply the extended arm of their principals, and ultimately they are therefore in need of legitimacy almost as much as elected politicians are. Such legitimacy cannot be sought exclusively in their particular skills and education (different from, say, lawyers or medical doctors); it has to be value-based and democratically grounded. This makes policy professionals vulnerable to various sorts of populist targeting, something to which I will return in the closing of this book.

POLITICAL POWER AND POLITICAL INEQUALITY

The last theme this book will cover is the role of policy professionals in the forging and use of political power, and in the connected issue of contemporary political inequality. To begin, we could discard one possible power problem connected to policy professionals. The democratic problem is *not* that they usurp power and disobey their principals. It is not the case that they have now become the secret power-holders of parties and organizations, behind the backs and against the interests of elected leaders and other principals. On the contrary, they tend to be loyal to their masters to the extent that the gulf between leaders and ordinary members risks becoming deeper and wider. Armed not only with their own superior knowledge but with support from the full gamut of their policy professionals' skills, organizational leaders become even more independent from their members' input or wishes than envisioned in Robert Michels' classical study of party leaders and followers (Michels 1911 [1962]). The behaviour of the disloyal staff members of Donald Trump, on which this book started, is anomalous and aberrational and not the standard fare when it comes to relations between organizational leadership and policy professionals.

The possible detrimental impact of policy professionalism should be sought elsewhere, in how it affects the forging and use of political power, in particular the complexity and visibility of political processes, and how it strengthens the links between economic and political inequality.

The work of policy professionals contributes to a complexity spiral in politics and policy making. As pointed out, they are brought in partly as a response to a more complex political environment, but far from reducing such complexity, their activities (in framing issues, using personal networks, or avoiding unwanted media attention) tend to increase political complexity even further. This in turn makes organized politics even harder for lay actors or the general public to understand or affect. The visibility of political processes decreases as power moves in networks and in informal shape, and as careers of resourceful actors span various organizations in the public and private spheres.

Politics in the policy professional guise therefore displays some disturbing similarities with pre-democratic modes of organizing political power. Now, as then, the 'royal court politics' of unelected political actors includes arcane and diffuse procedures taking place behind the official scene and beyond the public gaze. Now, as then, ways of recruitment and promotion are dependent on personal loyalties and value affinities. Now, as then, it is not clear whether it is the king or his loyal advisor who instigates political action and change. The Thomas Cromwells of yesteryear display some uncanny similarities with contemporary policy professionals, with the important proviso that advisors and other policy professionals today work in a highly organized and institutionalized setting. Perhaps future observers will come to see the period of mass-member organizations, electoral rule, independent public administrations, and clear-cut corporatist decision making and compromises as an historical exception, framed at both ends by more personalized, network-based, diffuse, and invisible forms of political power-making. The return of the mediaeval – although in a highly organized and democratic or post-democratic form – could possibly be one outcome of the rise of policy professionals.

The blurring of politics is evident also in the form of dissolving of the institutional boundaries between corporations/markets and the political sphere, and between civil society and politics. Through their networks and their careers, policy professionals span the boundaries between the economic and the political spheres, and between government and civil society organizations. They bring perspectives and techniques from one domain to the other, affecting government, business, and civil society organizations in the long run. The 'businessification' of politics runs parallel to the politicization of business and makes institutional spheres more similar to each other (Tyllström 2019). Similar processes occur among civil society organizations, which tend to become more and more professionalized and politically savvy in their influence work and less dependent on their members (Lang 2013, Walker 2014).

How future career options among policy professionals affect their current activities and strategies becomes a salient topic with particular relevance for those who move into and out of government offices. In their case, the main democratic worry is not that they would use old contacts for new attempts to influence; it is rather that their behaviour while still in public office may be affected by their future career plans and prospects. As shown in this book, the employment traffic between government offices and the lobbying industry as broadly defined is substantial, and the blurring of institutional spheres that it represents is a potential democratic problem.

A democratic problem also arises because policy professionalism is a quite expensive way to do politics, especially compared to relying on volunteers and part-time officials. The economic cost of hiring skilled professionals to do politics and affect policy making is substantial, regardless of whether such hiring is on a semi-permanent basis or varies from mission to mission. In turn, this means that the resource dependency feeds economic inequality into the political system and converts it into political inequality. In a time of sharply increasing economic inequalities in many countries, a tighter bond between economic and political inequality becomes particularly problematic.

From this point of view, the two separate problems identified by Dahl (1989: Ch. 23) as especially adverse to the future of political equality – rising economic inequality and the rise of knowledge-based and resourceful 'policy specialists' – are actually quite clearly linked. More economic resources allow the hiring of more savvy political specialists, and more savvy specialists can be used to better one's position in the battle for political dominance, which in turn affects the future distribution of resources. As argued by Hacker and Pierson, this amounts to quite strong feedback loops between economic distribution, organized political action to change or maintain this distribution, and public policies that strongly affect the distribution of resources (Hacker and Pierson 2010: Ch. 2, cf. Svallfors 2016).

The combined problems of low political visibility and high political inequality seem to be perfect recipe ingredients for fomenting angry populism. Policy professionals are 'the ideal enemy' for populism, especially right-wing populism, in more than one way. Not only do their activities contribute to political inequality and create the (not completely inaccurate) feeling that politics moves in the dark, that the real political decisions are taken far away from citizens' and voters' scrutiny. Policy professionals are also typically university educated, socially and culturally liberal, and move as insiders in the circles of power. In a word, they constitute, or can at least easily be painted as, the 'Establishment'. The repeated promises by populist leaders to 'drain the swamp' and get rid of the slick backroom operators are not restricted to Washington politics but are a standard ingredient of virtually all populist parties and movements (Müller 2016: Ch. 1).

Of course, such populist challenges rarely result in any true democratization or 'draining of the swamp'. Instead, populist leaders tend to bring in their own policy professionals to do their bidding; the swamp is not drained but merely filled with new creatures. In the extreme cases of the successful establishment of authoritarian control, policy professionals are completely cut loose from democratic supervision and become dependent only on the political leader's acceptance and support. The Putin cronies our introductory chapter saw 'trying to divine the intentions of their leader' need not concern themselves much with citizens or voters, only with Vlad's wishes and worries (Zygar 2017: 346).

A true democratization of policy professionalism would have to include quite different means of bringing out the democratic potential of policy professionals and offsetting their possible detrimental effects for democracy and political equality. Policy professionals will remain a salient feature of any advanced democracy, and the question is how could their activities be made to work for and not against democracy. Any detailed programme in this regard would fall far beyond the scope of this book and would also need to be carefully tailored to particular circumstances in specific polities. Two aspects of any such reforms could nevertheless be emphasized: they should attempt to *block political exchanges* that are detrimental to political equality, and they should *level the political playing field* as much as possible.

The notion of 'blocked exchanges' comes from political philosopher Michael Walzer and his *Spheres of Justice* (Walzer 1983). The basic idea here is that inequalities in one particular domain should not be allowed to spill over into other domains; for example, injustice appears when differences in incomes spill over into inequalities in life expectancy. Or in our case, injustice appears when economic inequality strengthens political inequality or vice versa. Such blocked exchanges are of course easier to define than to achieve, but a couple of ideas could be ventured. One is that unrestricted exchange of personnel between institutional spheres constitutes a democratic problem. Incumbents of government positions may let their personal career plans affect their current course of action, and insider information can travel in ways that put the wider public at great disadvantage. In many countries, partial or full embargos on moving between government and private firms have therefore been implemented. In order to be effective, such embargos should probably be narrowly defined as including only issues in which the incumbent has been directly involved. To give an example, the political advisor who worked for the department of health should not be allowed to move directly to the health care industry, but could well move to, say, the building industry. Such partial embargos are standard in private business employment contracts and should be feasible also for the movements between government and lobbying.

In order to decrease the impact of economic resources on political inequality, a broad repertoire of measures are available, including public funding support for political parties and other democratic organizations, restrictions, and open information regarding private funding of such organizations, and limits on spending for political purposes. Many of these measures have been implemented in many countries, but more can surely be done in many places. In our case, the intended effect of such measures is to hinder differences in economic resources to be translated into differences in the degree to which political expertise can be bought in the policy professional labour market.

So funding options and limitations are one way to block exchanges between economics and politics, but they also may contribute to levelling the playing field for various parties and organizations. A further contribution to levelling the playing field should be sought in access to information. The existence of an impartial public administration with a high capacity for independent analyses certainly contributes to making the framing attempts and the information advantage of policy professionals less influential, as does the quality and reach of public service news media and other forms of independent high-quality journalism. Such independent sources of information and analyses need to be strengthened (or in the current climate, defended) in order to provide as good information equality as possible.

An important first step, and one to which this book has hopefully contributed, is to better understand and communicate what the real world of politics and policy making actually looks like. The standard political science textbook still contains precious little about what the whole new world of policy professionalism entails (Garsten, Rothstein, and Svallfors 2015: 12–14). Analyses such as the present one should form the basis for a different way to present the study of politics to students and the public. Such a broader and alternative presentation needs to go beyond fictions about the 'parliamentary steering chain', and beyond assumptions of political equality between citizens. It would need to consider politics and policy making as being basically action among highly organized actors, conducted by skilled professionals, highly unequal in terms of influence, and subject to the impact of economic and cognitive resources that are highly inegalitarian in their distribution. Only by looking political reality squarely in the eye is it possible to eventually shift it in a more democratic and egalitarian direction, and political and social science need to do a better job in this regard.

NOTE

1. Quoted from Robert A. Caro's *Master of the Senate. (The Years of Lyndon Johnson, Vol 3)*. New York: Vintage Books, 2002, p. 382.

REFERENCES

Achen, Christopher H., and Larry M. Bartels. 2016. *Democracy for Realists. Why Elections Do Not Produce Responsive Government*. Princeton, NJ: Princeton University Press.
Barley, Stephen, and Gideon Kunda. 2004. *Gurus, Hired Guns, and Warm Bodies: Itinerant Experts in a Knowledge Economy*. Princeton, NJ: Princeton University Press.
Brennan, Jason. 2016. *Against Democracy*. Princeton, NJ: Princeton University Press.
Croitoru, Alin. 2012. 'Schumpeter, J.A., 1934 (2008), The Theory of Economic Development: An Inquiry into Profits, Capital, Credit, Interest and the Business Cycle. A review to a book that is 100 years old.' *Journal of Comparative Research in Anthropology and Sociology* 3 (2): 137–48.
Dahl, Robert A. 1989. *Democracy and Its Critics*. New Haven, CT: Yale University Press.
Dahlström, Carl, and Victor Lapuente. 2017. *Organizing Leviathan. Politicians, Bureaucrats, and the Making of Good Government*. Cambridge: Cambridge University Press.
Garsten, Christina, Bo Rothstein, and Stefan Svallfors. 2015. *Makt utan mandat. De policyprofessionella i svensk politik*. Stockholm: Dialogos.
Hacker, Jacob S., and Paul Pierson. 2010. *Winner-Take-All Politics: How Washington Made the Rich Richer – and Turned Its Back on the Middle Class*. New York: Simon & Schuster.
Harrington, Brooke. 2016. *Capital without Borders: Wealth Managers and the One Percent*. Cambridge, MA: Harvard University Press.
Holst, Cathrine, and Anders Molander. 2019. 'Epistemic Democracy and the Role of Experts.' *Contemporary Political Theory* 18 (4): 541–61, doi: 10.1057/s41296-018-00299-4.
Lang, Sabine. 2013. *NGOs, Civil Society, and the Public Sphere*. New York: Cambridge University Press.

Lundquist, Lennart. 1998. *Demokratins väktare: ämbetsmännen och vårt offentliga etos*. Lund: Studentlitteratur.

Michels, Robert. 1911. *Political Parties: A Sociological Study of the Oligarchical Tendencies of Modern Democracy*. Reprinted in 1962. New York: Free Press.

Müller, Jan-Werner. 2016. *What is Populism?* London: Penguin Books.

Noordegraaf, Mirko, Martijn van der Steen, and Mark van Twist. 2014. 'Fragmented or Connective Professionalism? Strategies for Professionalizing the Work of Strategists and Other (Organizational) Professionals.' *Public Administration* 92 (1): 21–38.

Rothstein, Bo. 2019. 'Epistemic Democracy and the Quality of Government.' *European Politics and Society* 20 (1): 16–31.

Steinmo, Sven. 2012. 'Governing as an Engineering Problem: The Political Economy of Swedish Success.' In *Politics in the Age of Austerity*, edited by Armin Schäfer and Wolfgang Streeck, pp. 84–107. Cambridge, UK: Polity Press.

Svallfors, Stefan. 2016. 'Politics as Organized Combat – New Players and New Rules of the Game in Sweden.' *New Political Economy* 21 (6): 505–19.

Tyllström, Anna. 2019. 'More Than a Revolving Door: Corporate Lobbying and the Socialization of Institutional Carriers.' *Organization Studies*, https://doi.org/10.1177/0170840619848014.

Walker, Edward T. 2014. *Grassroots for Hire. Public Affairs Consultants in American Democracy*. New York: Cambridge University Press.

Walzer, Michael. 1983. *Spheres of Justice. A Defence of Pluralism & Equality*. Oxford: Blackwell.

Weber, Max. 1919. 'Politik som yrke.' Reprinted in 1977, *Vetenskap och politik*, edited by Max Weber, pp. 40–95. Göteborg: Korpen.

Zygar, Michail. 2017. *All the Kremlin's Men. Inside the Court of Valdimir Putin*. New York: Public Affairs.

Methods appendix

The data on which this book builds stem from several sources, and in this appendix I will describe the data and analyses that are used in the book. The research projects on which the book is based have collected additional data of various sorts (Garsten, Rothstein, and Svallfors 2015: 273–93), but here I describe only data and analyses that are actually used in the book.

THE SWEDISH DATA 2012–18

Mapping

The data collection started with a quantitative mapping of Swedish policy professionals in 2012 (including 1468 individuals), containing descriptive information about gender, age, education, and labour market experience. Information from this mapping was collected mainly from open web sources complemented with a small-scale survey to local and regional political secretaries. This mapping also constituted the sampling frame for the subsequent research interviews.

In order to create a complete roster of Swedish policy professionals, relevant organizational types were first selected. Seven 'habitats' for policy professionals were identified: the government offices (Regeringskansliet), parliament (Riksdagen), trade unions, other major interest organizations, think tanks, PR firms (lobbying firms), and regional and local party offices. Note that this selection does not include in-house corporate lobbyists and representatives of smaller interest groups. Although they may be considered policy professionals for all intents and purposes, their organizations were deemed either too narrow or too peripheral to warrant inclusion.

In the second step, my research team catalogued all organizations of these seven habitats. We started by surveying the member associations of LO, SACO, TCO, and the Confederation of Swedish Enterprise – the three Swedish trade union federations and the main employers' organization in the country. As for PR and lobbying firms, the trade association of the PR and communications consultancy sector, PRECIS, publicly discloses its member companies.[1] Last, we tracked down think tanks through extensive web searches. To ensure full coverage, we analysed participation at the Almedalen Week, an annual political event which has become the most important public forum in Sweden.

In 2012, close to a thousand organizations attended the Almedalen Week.[2] This list of attendees served as a cross-check and revealed that no relevant organization had been omitted.

In the last step, we identified the policy professionals by accessing the websites of the organizations. For a person to be included in the population, three criteria had to be fulfilled: (1) the person is not elected into office but employed; (2) his or her main task is to craft and/or communicate policy; (3) this is done on a partisan basis to promote certain values and interests over others. Examples of such positions are communication strategist, public affairs manager, lobbyist, press secretary, political appointee, policy expert, and political advisor. In addition to the web-based mapping we also used a short survey given to local and regional political secretaries asking for similar information to that obtained from web sources.

During the spring of 2018, the occupational trajectories of policy professionals between 2012 and 2018 were coded via extensive web searches. After excluding the regional and local political secretaries to focus on the national level, 913 individuals in the 2012 sample were included. We were able to map the complete trajectories of 788 individuals. The remaining 125 had either retired or provided no information. The primary source of data was LinkedIn, the world's largest professional network with more than 562 million users.[3] On this online platform, people publish their resumes. These were downloaded and coded. In cases of missing data on LinkedIn, we followed their careers by means of press releases, news articles, websites of organizations, and personal websites. This is also the method by which we sought to cross-check the information disclosed on LinkedIn. Whenever somebody joined another organization or changed position within the same organization, a new record was created and inserted into the database. This record stores information on position, organization, and employment commencement date.

A guiding principle throughout this coding was to retain as much information as possible while enabling the aggregation into larger categories. To do so, we first devised codes representing types of organizations. These do not merely encompass the six types of organizations but cover all possible destinations for policy professionals, including but not limited to the private sector, public agencies, media, European Union, interest organizations (not part of the sampling frame), and universities and research institutes. Next, we created an occupational classification system. If multiple titles were identical for essentially the same occupation, they were registered under the same code. For example, the role of both policy experts in organizations and political advisors in the government is to formulate policies. In a similar vein, press secretaries, media relations officers, and information coordinators – no matter which organizations they work for – received the same occupational code. It is important to acknowledge that titles can be misleading. Therefore, when in doubt, we read job descriptions to ensure that the designated code truly reflected the nature of the employment. This is also how we established whether a change of title was merely a formality or if someone was indeed assigned new responsibilities within the same organization. Only if the day-to-day responsibilities changed did we add a new record. Ultimately, this system of codes allowed us to split and aggregate policy professionals according to their organizations and their functions and to observe the flows into, out of, and within the policy professional field. Data from the mapping exercises were used in fairly basic descriptive statistics, to provide an overview of Swedish policy professionals' careers. We decided that the data were not of a kind to warrant more advanced quantitative analyses.

Interviews

A number of policy professionals were selected from the data base, and in 2012–13 our research assistants conducted long (average interview time is about 2.5 hours) semi-structured interviews with 71 of them. Interviewees were strategically selected in order to cover a broad span in terms of age, gender, and professional experiences, as well as different positions and occupational types. In this respect, the sampling aims to maximize variability within the category rather than to constitute a representative sample of Swedish policy professionals. In addition, 21 shorter interviews (about one hour each) were conducted with elected politicians (MPs and former government ministers), (newly retired) civil servants, recruiters, and policy professionals working for private enterprises. Table A.1 provides an overview of the interviewees and their distribution across organizational types. Interviews were transcribed (about 3500 pages), and pertinent interview quotes were assembled in a 100-page excerpt document (in Swedish, available from the author).

The interviews were designed to cover three main topics: (1) the work of policy professionals as a specific form of political influence; (2) the occupation and career choices of policy professionals; and (3) the labour market for policy professionals. For each topic, a number of themes were covered in order to provide a comprehensive picture of the work and careers of policy professionals in Sweden. The interview guide (in Swedish) is available on request.

A subsample of the interviewees from this first round were re-interviewed in 2018 (N = 32). These interviews were again semi-structured, but this time the focus was on the interviewees' careers since 2012 and their considerations in this regard. The selection of re-interviewees was strategic in order to cover those who had *remained* in the same job since 2012, those who had *moved* to other policy professional positions in the field, and those who had *exited* from the policy professional field.

Table A.1   Sweden: interviewees (2012–13). Informants (2013)

Organizational type	Men	Women	Total
Government Offices	8	4	12
Parliamentary Party Office	5	7	12
Local/Regional	6	7	13
Trade Union	5	8	13
Interest Organization	6	3	9
Think Tank	3	2	5
Public Affairs/Lobbying Firm	5	2	7
Total	**38**	**33**	**71**
(Former) Government Minister	3	1	4
MPs	4	2	6
(Retired) Civil Servants	1	1	2
Recruiters	5	1	6
Private Companies	3	0	3
Total	**16**	**5**	**21**

All interviews were recorded, transcribed verbatim, and coded for pertinent themes. The final result of this exercise for the 2018 interviews is a 48-page thematic excerpt document (in Swedish, available on request), from which all quotes in the book have been selected and translated.

Interviews with Private Welfare Lobbyists

The empirical case in Chapter 6 is based on seven interviews conducted in 2016 with key organizational representatives of the private health care sector in order to decide what types of actions private firms and their organizations use in their lobbying efforts. The interview guide (in Swedish) is available on request. The interviews were recorded and transcribed verbatim. Pertinent interview quotes were collected in an excerpt document (in Swedish, available on request), from which the quotes used in Chapter 6 stem.

THE COMPARATIVE DATA

In order to put the national Swedish data in perspective, my research team also conducted interviews with Swedish policy professionals in Brussels, working in the European Parliament or as part of the lobbying scene around the EU institutions. These interviews were conducted in 2015–16. We also did

Table A.2   Brussels: interviewees (2015–16)

Organizational type	Men	Women	Total
Parliamentary Party Office	5	4	9
Regional Lobbyists	2	2	4
Trade Union	2		2
Interest Organization	4	3	7
Public Affairs/Lobbying Firm	5		5
Total	**18**	**9**	**27**

Note: In addition, one Swedish MEP was interviewed.

interviews in Ireland, Latvia, and the Netherlands in 2016–18. These interviews were conducted in English. The interview guides for the comparative interviews were closely matched with the original Swedish interviews to allow systematic comparison between contexts, but small amendments to fit local circumstances were of course necessary. The interview guides (in Swedish or English) are available on request.

The samples of interviews in all four contexts were strategically chosen, covering a broad span in terms of age, gender, and professional experiences, as well as different positions and occupational types. The interview sample in Brussels was made by choosing strategically from lists of political secretaries in the European Parliament and from the lobbying registers of the European Commission. The interview samples for the three contrasting country cases were constructed from lists of relevant policy professional positions compiled by an MSc student in each country, working with instructions from me.

As shown in Tables A.2 and A.3, due to institutional differences between these contrasting contexts and the Swedish one, the interview samples differ somewhat in their composition from the original Swedish sample. There are no government offices at the EU level – the Commission is a different kind of body than regular government offices – hence no such Swedish political advisors are included in the sample. And there are no specific Swedish think tanks to sample from at the European level. Among the three country cases, nowhere else than in Sweden do we find trade unions and employer federations having strong analytical capacities. Hence, we decided to choose interviewees from the four remaining organizational types. As far as can be judged, these differences in sample constructions are unlikely to bias results in any substantive way.

Table A.3   *Ireland, Latvia, the Netherlands: interviewees (2016–18)*

Organizational type	Ireland	Latvia	Netherlands
Government Offices	3	4	3
Parliamentary Party Office	8	4	5
Think Tank	3	2	5
Public Affairs/Lobbying Firm	5	4	7
Total	**19**	**14**	**20**
(% women)	**(37)**	**(64)**	**(55)**

CODING AND ANALYSES

All interviews were recorded, transcribed verbatim, and coded for pertinent themes. The thematic analysis followed an abductive format, in which sets of categories derived from the main research questions were subsequently revised in a stepwise fashion through confrontation with salient interview quotes and through input from research project members. The original categories were thus amended, collapsed, or split, and new categories were introduced to cover pertinent interview themes. The final result of this exercise is a number of thematic excerpt documents (in Swedish or English, available on request), from which all quotes in this book have been selected and (if they were in Swedish) translated.

The coding of themes has been a collective exercise, in which I have had the main responsibility, but where my collaborators have provided input to scrutinize and question preliminary codings. In this way, we attempted not to be overly guided by a single (and possibly sometimes mistaken) analyst. The fact that most participants in both projects conducted some of the interviews themselves and also used transcripts and excerpt documents for their own analyses provides further safeguards against excessive subjectivity in selection and interpretation.

LIMITATIONS AND ALTERNATIVES

Relying mainly on interviews brings both advantages and important limitations. The long thematic interviews allowed nuances to be articulated, and it provided strikingly frank and open discussion of various aspects of the work of policy professionals (provided under guarantees of anonymity). At the same time, one must take into account the self-understanding of the interviewees, who may easily exaggerate or underestimate their own role in politics and policy making. However, the interviews with (ex-)politicians, civil servants, and organizational recruiters served as important addenda to the interviews with policy professionals. In general, these additional interviews confirmed what had transpired from the main interviews, that is, that the interviewees' representation of what, how, and why they do what they do is shared by groups who come into regular contact with them. One should note, however, that these additional interviews were largely confined to Sweden (including one Swedish MEP), so that such 'checks' are not available for the other countries.

Alternative strategies for eliciting information would certainly have been possible. Two obvious candidates are reliance on survey data (i.e., Yong and Hazell 2014) and the use of direct observations (i.e., Rhodes, 't Hart, and Noordegraaf 2007). We decided against the first strategy for two reasons. First, because we thought it would be next to impossible to achieve an acceptable response rate with this group of busy people, and second, because we originally knew too little about the category in question to formulate clear-cut survey questions that would really tap into the essence of their work.

The difference between our approach and using more direct observations should not be exaggerated. All observation studies rely on interviews and conversation in order to make sense of observations, and virtually all our interviews were conducted in a work setting. The difference is more a question of emphasis and nuance. We opted for interviews in order to be able to cover a broader span of organizational types and positions. Direct observation is a very time-consuming strategy, which in practice limits its application to a few particular settings or even specific individuals (Rhodes 2011, Rhodes, 't Hart, and Noordegraaf 2007).

RESEARCH ETHICS AND DATA AVAILABILITY

All interviews adhered to relevant laws and ethical guidelines, and the project was vetted and approved by the regional research ethics board in Stockholm. Interviews were held under the conditions of informed consent and preserved anonymity of the interviewees. Interviewees were informed that their participation was entirely voluntary, that they could withdraw cooperation at any point, that data were to be used only for research purposes, and that their identity would be protected in publications and data sharing. Interviewees were invited to read their transcripts and amend these if necessary (very few ever used that option). In the book, the anonymity of respondents has been preserved, in a few cases by changing small insignificant pieces of information or using more generic job titles than their specific ones.

Interviews, transcripts, data files, and other sensitive data are kept on a secure server at the Institute for Futures Studies. Printed transcripts are kept in a locked safe. Before the end of the year 2020, a redacted version (excluding all identifiable information about interviewees and the organizations) of interview transcripts will be made available for future research. All interview guides and excerpt documents are available from me on request.

NOTES

1. http://www.precis.se/list-of-members/ (accessed 15 September 2015).
2. http://program.almedalsveckan.info/12444 (accessed 10 January 2014).
3. https://about.linkedin.com/ (accessed 26 September 2018).

REFERENCES

Garsten, Christina, Bo Rothstein, and Stefan Svallfors. 2015. *Makt utan mandat. De policyprofessionella i svensk politik.* Stockholm: Dialogos.
Rhodes, R.A.W. 2011. *Everyday Life in British Government.* Oxford/New York: Oxford University Press.
Rhodes, R.A.W., Paul 't Hart, and Mirko Noordegraaf, eds. 2007. *Observing Government Elites. Up Close and Personal.* Basingstoke: Palgrave Macmillan.
Yong, Ben, and Robert Hazell. 2014. *Special Advisers: Who They Are, What They Do and Why They Matter.* Oxford: Hart.

Index